MW01104780

ENCYCLOPEDIA for THE NEW AMERICAN CENTURY

ENCYCLOPEDIA for THE NEW AMERICAN CENTURY

✦

Understanding Verbalizations in this New Age of Empire, Mythology and Consumerism.

R.B. Vineyard

iUniverse, Inc.
New York Lincoln Shanghai

ENCYCLOPEDIA for THE NEW AMERICAN CENTURY
Understanding Verbalizations in this New Age of Empire, Mythology and Consumerism.

iUniverse books may be ordered through booksellers or by contacting:

iUniverse
2021 Pine Lake Road, Suite 100
Lincoln, NE 68512
www.iuniverse.com
1-800-Authors (1-800-288-4677)

ISBN-13: 978-0-595-38697-0 (pbk)
ISBN-13: 978-0-595-83080-0 (ebk)
ISBN-10: 0-595-38697-0 (pbk)
ISBN-10: 0-595-83080-3 (ebk)

Printed in the United States of America

Contents

Get over it! The New American Century has started with or without you. Get with it! It's time for everyone to get in line and join in the new unity and spirit of uni-partisanship—or else! The first step in knowing what's expected of you is to understand the language of dittoheadedness, neo-conformism, neo-speak and good old ass kissing of the properly imposed authorities. You might as well join up because if you don't you're against it and that makes you a terrorist. Let the doubters and scoffers chafe against the inevitable tide of empire. The smart thing to do is to go meekly with the flow, for the meek shall inherit the earth!

As it is theoretically possible for every soul to be redeemed, so too is it possible for the liberal to reach within his or her self and nurture that strain of unenlightened selfishness so necessary in order to navigate the jungles of modern American life. Throw out the old morality for it is not nearly old enough. Learn that what you thought was good is bad and that what you thought was bad is good. Think not that this is a perversion of reality. Rather, it is the new normalcy, the new social and political environment designed to carry us all into the end of times. We are at the threshold of a quickening, a choosing of sides, a race to the finish in which there will be winners and there will be losers. Don the cloak of self-righteousness and join the winning party. Cast off your integrity and your critical eye—these are impediments to your happiness. Align your self worth to military conquest—that will more than compensate for any self-esteem issues. Let denial be a virtue—not the denial of earthly possessions, God forbid!—But denial of the humanity of those who think and act differently. Allow yourself to be delivered into a delicious frenzy of disdain by the preachers of the New American Century. Yes, look at the world only through the lens of the corporate controlled mass media. Know that as an AMERICAN you are blessed above all and the envy of all and because of this *they* despise you and so deserve to be despised in kind. Have no doubts but submit your heart and mind to fear, for in fear you will truly be alive, motivated, willing and able to accept security at all costs. Above all, to your own self be deceitful.

Everyone has a vital role to play in America's magnificent future. The young and able-bodied are destined for glorious conquests, carrying the torch of American liberty, freedom and dominion to exotic climes and locations. The vast majority of the lesser born—those too old or feeble to contribute to pushing the boundaries of state—they will enjoy the fruits of their labor, industry, diligence and duty, for they are the folks back home, mom and dad, the children of the Heartland. They are the wellspring upon whose backs the corporate state must rely on to man the factories, work the mines, raise up the sons and daughters of the Pentagon and above all, buy without question or hesitation. And from these teeming masses will rise a few to the very feet of the gods—those gifted with special talents, the artists, entertainers, those with a genius for communicating the blessings of Pax Americana to all the nations. These few will taste of the largess of the wellborn and will surely be an inspiration to their lowly brethren.

So come! Utopia is at hand. Freedom, while it certainly comes from the barrel of a gun, also comes with the knowledge that your neighbor is just like you and his neighbor is just like him and so it goes as far as the eye can see and the eagle can soar. GOD BLESS AMERICA!

A is for AMERICA

Abortion: An abominable practice invented by feminists whose underlying motive is one of convenience to alleviate them from the responsibility of parenthood. As with everything, there is always an exception to the rule. Pro-Life women may obtain abortions with a clear conscience as long as they are discreet or spend a respectable time publicly repenting of it. Secrecy is best, but if you have to confess, a few Hail Mary's or a forgive-me-Jesus will get you over the hump. One can also say that it was a miscarriage.

As for those teens that find themselves with a bun in the oven, you have to ask your mommy or daddy to get an abortion. Tough luck if it's daddy's! Just remember though, once you do get an abortion you can never take it back and it will haunt you all your living days. If not, the Christian Coalition will.

There are places semi-technically in America (like Saipan) where you can get a forced abortion if you're one of the lucky girls to have emigrated there in search of the American dream.

Someday, all abortions will become illegal except for the rich who can afford to go out of the country or to "quiet" clinics. For the rest, "back alley" abortions will always be in vogue.

Abramoff, Jack: Influential lobbyist and Majority Whip Tom DeLay's travel agent. This incredible money making machine actually used an Indian tribe's money to finance a Focus on the Family crusade against gambling in order to shut down a rival tribe's casino! But, uh-oh! Abramoff has been playing fast and loose for far too long and now has copped to many a guilty plea with the result that at least a score of our fine lawmakers are quaking in their boots! Not to fear, heading up the prosecution is none other than Alice Fisher, Bush recess appointee with no prosecutorial experience but plenty of right wing connections to make up for it!

Abstinence: The act of not sharing disgusting, disease-ridden juices with others. That, of course, is for the children (and one would like to think priests and gays). Teaching abstinence only in schools is today's sex education. Whereas children

1

were being equipped with knowledge far and beyond that of their parents, which ostensibly led to all sorts of debauchery, today's youth are to be scared limp by tales of horror and filth. Of course, the kids see through the hype instantly and go about their debauchery with a newly aroused curiosity and ignorance. In fact, some of the numbers are in and it appears that those who pledge to abstain and declare virginity until marriage are more likely to engage in unprotected oral and anal sex! It appears that **A**bstinence **I**nvites **D**eviant **S**ex! No matter, Abstinence Only education is the moral thing to do and no amount of statistics or human behavior can change that.

Abu Ghraib: Detention camp for Iraqi detainees. Also, a resort for military police where they can engage in fraternity type pranks and blow off some steam. As with Las Vegas, what goes on in Abu Ghraib should stay in Abu Ghraib. If not, however, let the world know that America expects its own to be treated under the rules as put forward by the Geneva Convention.

Abuse of Power: The use of one's position to benefit the underclass to the detriment of the well heeled is totally an abuse of power. Also, using long standing Senate rules in order to thwart the will and wishes of those promoting the New American Century is an absolute abuse of power! Such rules are arcane and must be sent to the dustbin of history. While they served a useful purpose in the past by protecting the minority against the tyranny of the majority, in the future no minority will be acknowledged and therefore there will be nothing to protect.

Access: The right of the rich and powerful to influence government officials. Access is granted in direct proportion to campaign contributions and the like. A well-placed contribution will put one way ahead of a US Senator on the fast track to the Oval Office as seen by "Kenny Boy" Lay's frequent luncheons with the President while California Senator Barbara Boxer rightfully got the brush off.

Accountability: Accountability is accepting the praise for anything good you have done and righteously laying the blame on someone else for misdeeds, errors or acts of outright criminality (regardless who is the true guilty party). Of course, from a position of power it is possible to hold no one accountable for anything by ignoring the charge and suppressing the news. (See also Responsibility)

Accounting: Accounting is record keeping of business transactions. Companies involved in nation building overseas are exempt from such practices while companies that are proponents of the New American Century may use "artistic" accounting practices as long as they don't draw undue attention to themselves.

ACLU: American Communist Lawyers Union. This gang of creeps is guaranteed to show up whenever anybody gets their precious ego bruised or to defend indefensible un-American traitorous acts. That being said, the ACLU is an invaluable aid to proponents of the New American Century because they are so easy to despise. They are useful in demonizing lawyers and help the public understand what they are supposed to be against, namely, everything the ACLU is for (the Bill of Rights). One thing about the ACLU though, if the government decides to trammel on *your* civil rights they will go to bat for you no matter who you are. (See Rush Limbaugh)

Actions: As the old saw goes, "Actions speak louder than words." For the fearless leaders, of America, the shakers and movers, it all depends. Sometimes words speak louder than actions. In such instances one should "do as I say, not as I do." Take, for instance, our newfound love for torturing suspected terrorists. Now, this is plainly **not** an invitation for nations to go around torturing people other than their own. This is merely a declaration that America reserves the right to nudge some information out of captured enemy combatants and America would be very angry with anyone who would dare torture a captured serviceman.

Activist Judges: Any interpretation of the law that goes against the American people—that is, that goes against the tenets of the New American Century—is an act and therefore is enacted by Activist Judges who must be counteracted by inactive judges from the Federalist Society and/or their blessed kind.

Advertising: The art of convincing the public what to buy and when in total disregard of their own best interests. The sire of Public Relations.

Affordable Housing: Available due to liberal laws that are designed to ruin neighborhoods and lower housing values. Why don't we just have affordable everything? Then everyone can drive a Bentley on their own personal payment plan! Affordable housing is the first step on the slippery slope to communism.

Age Discrimination: Old timers get to ride buses, dine, go to movies at reduced rates and get all sorts of other perks simply because they are youthfully challenged. It's not fair. Old people get paid and don't even work for it. The young people have to pay for *their* leisure. That's certainly not fair! So maybe it's high time the young people take their money and invest it in themselves and not the old people.

Incidentally, we've heard of complaints by old timers that they sometimes get bumped from certain jobs just because they're ancient. Should we let octogenarians play pro football? Is that it? Perhaps they'd like to join the army. Let's get real and get rid of all this discrimination nonsense altogether. Back in the old days—when all these whining old timers were young, by the way—they didn't put up with anyone nitpicking about age, sex, or racial discrimination. They, by golly, didn't stand for it one bit! So let's move forward and go back to the times when all this crap didn't exist. Back to the times when you knew your place and if you had a beef you either liked it or lumped it.

Agenda: A nice businesslike term for one's plans. Liberals, free thinkers, communists and all other types of evildoers like to co-opt this word. However, they do not really have agendas. They plot and scheme and connive their outrageous conspiracies in iniquitous dens.

Agent Orange: A fine example of better warfare through chemistry—Agent Orange is a premium defoliant and cancer-causing agent. Agent orange is responsible for transforming much of Vietnam's useless jungles into wide savannahs and many a GI into a carcinogenic slagheap.

Since Iraq is not known for its jungles, our chemical of choice in that area is depleted uranium.

Agent Provocateurs: Young Republicans or others loyal to the cause placed at demonstrations to throw rocks at the police to give them an excuse to riot on the protesters.

Agnostic: A fancy-pants way of not admitting that one is an atheist. Agnostics claim that there is a God but don't know who He is. Can't they read?

Imagine being so confused that one does not have a personal relationship with his or her own maker! Why, that might just give one leave to go and invent an entire worldview that doesn't jibe with the real one we've been given. It's cosmic anarchy, plain and simple! How in the world can we expect everyone to hold all our traditional values dear if people just go off and believe anything they like? It's wussy, feel good theology, dreamt up by folks who can't take the fire and brimstone, the down to earth reality of Jehovah God! Well, if they can't believe in God, by God then they better fear going to Hell!

AIDS: An industry unto itself. AIDS is believed to be the wrath of God on the immoral, the abominable and the non-white. It also serves a useful purpose in promoting abstinence. As well, any number of debilitating conditions can be construed as AIDS thus creating a fierce market for exotic and costly medications.

AIPAC: The American Israel Public Affairs Committee, a.k.a. the tail that wags the dogs of Washington. There's a lot of hype these days about Israeli influence in America. Since we were founded on the Judeo-Christian ethic, it would seem that folks would actually feel good about it but alas, that isn't so. If only Texas were the Promised Land. Then we could have it both ways.

Air America Radio: Here's a freakish idea that will never work—liberal radio! Oh, sure, although they've been broadcasting for a little over a year and are cleaning up in the Neilson ratings in every market but that's just because people are curious and maybe a little bored of the standard fair. One has to ask if one could listen live on www.airamericaradio.com anywhere in the world, why would they want to when they can listen to Rush and let him do all their thinking for them? Who are these people? OK, a few names like Al Franken, Jerry Springer, Randi Rhodes and Robert F. Kennedy, Jr. So what?

Alexander The Great (356–323 BC): People today just don't appreciate how much this guy influences us. Back in the day he was real, real big, having spread Greek culture throughout a wide chunk of Asia and North Africa and all by the time he was 33. The New Testament was written in Greek, for Christ's sake!

One interesting little story concerns Alexander's statement that "If I were not Alexander, I should wish to be Diogenes". Now, when the two met, Diogenes was living like a bum in a big empty tub. He was sunbathing when Alexander introduced himself and asked if he could do anything for the older man. Diogenes said he could move out of the way, for he was blocking his sun. Thus, one must conclude that Alexander "wished" he were Diogenes not because he wanted to be a penniless bum but that he admired his chutzpah. This demonstrates Alexander's greatness—or at least his extraordinary distinction from his contemporaries—as any other world-conquering hero of the times would probably have lopped off the old man's head for his insolence.

Alien: Anyone unlucky enough to be born outside of America. Excluding white aliens from English speaking or Teutonic nations, aliens are unwelcome in America unless they'll either do things nobody else will for slave wages or will vociferously denounce their former country. With today's technology and Free Trade, aliens are welcome to stay where they are and do the same jobs lower class Americans do for a fraction of the wages and under who knows and who cares what conditions.

Space aliens will be the next peril to national security after the Muslim and Asian threats run their course.

Alien Tort Claims Act of 1789: Enacted by the First Congress and signed into law by none other than George Washington himself, this strange law lay fallow for 200 years before some do-gooding, busybody, anti-business creeps dusted it off and began using it to sue American corporations doing business overseas. Originally, the law was passed because a few American pirates were causing a stink and we didn't want some stupid state court to rile a foreign nation so it was made a federal law in order for foreign grievances to be heard in federal courts only. Now it's come back to bite some very fine corporations working abroad. Some ask, what's the use of going overseas to escape American law if it's just going to follow you around? It does have a chilling effect on being able to take advantage of the lack of local statutes.

Alito, Samuel: Bush's swing vote nominee to the Supreme Court following the Miers debacle. Judge Alito is a supremely qualified nominee (inasmuch as he believes in the godlike powers of the Presidency and understands Congress to be the impediment that it is) who will take the ball running for the New American Century and will help remold the judicial landscape for years to come. If there is any flaw in this great American is that he, like several others on the bench is Catholic and not a straight shooting fundamentalist real Christian.

Al Jazeera: One of the premier Arabic news stations in the Middle East. Located in Qatar, Al Jazeera has maintained a fierce independence, often airing news items embarrassing to neighboring countries. That's good. But Al Jazeera also likes to show what's going on in Iraq. That puts it and its reporters on very shaky ground with America.

Al Qaeda: The heart and soul of all terrorism in the world today, responsible for the horrendous events of 9/11. If it's nasty either Al Qaeda did it or at least approves of it.

Al Qaeda is an international network of crazed Islamic militants bent on destroying outside influences to the Muslim world. Because its membership does not belong to a single country nor does any one government overtly sponsor it, Al Qaeda is nothing more than a fanatical religious based NGO.

Alternative Medicine: Any heretical practice that is not sanctioned by the AMA or the pharmaceutical companies is "alternative", i.e., quackery and outright criminality. Alternative medicine threatens the profits of the entire medical industry. Along with preventative medicine and herbalism, alternative medicine should be abolished as witchcraft. (See the Codex Alimentarius Commission).

Altruism: Busybody do-gooderism affected by simpering, wimpy, high-minded, bleeding hearted people who feel good about themselves for being sympathetic to others. The road to Hell is paved with the bones of altruistic fools.

Ayn Rand was particularly crazed at altruistic acts. While a million other things drove her mad, altruism was probably in her top twenty. She is quoted as saying, "Every major horror of history was committed in the name of an altruistic motive. Has any act of selfishness ever equalled the carnage perpetrated by disciples of altruism?" Oh, it's so true! Think of Caesar lovingly striving to free the Gauls of their barbarism. Remember Hitler, hoping to free the world from the impending horrors of Armeggeddon by extinguishing the major players, thus nullifying the prophecy. Alexander, Genghis Kahn, the Vikings, the Conquistadores—all acting out of perverse altruism to wreak their unwitting damage upon the world.

Ambiguity: A useful quality of any public official. No ambiguous statement can be used against a person to impugn their integrity since it covers more than one meaning. To quote Condoleezza Rice when confronted with statements she made concerning WMD's she replied, "I have to say that I have never, ever, lost respect for the truth in the service of anything." On the surface Ms. Rice was defending her integrity but more subtly it may be interpreted to be an admission that she actually has no respect for the truth—you can't lose what you don't have. Or, she may have been admitting to having respect for the truth but simply does not employ it since her statement did not say, "I never *lied* in the service of anything." Moreover, she may have lost respect for the truth in the service of *some-*

thing, not just *any*thing. So, good for Condi. Her ambiguous skills are world class.

Ambition: The drive to improve one's self. Ambition is quite suitable for everyone as long as it is held within reasonable bounds of one's class.

> *"Don Quixote thought he could have made beautiful bird-cages and toothpicks if his brain had not been so full of ideas of chivalry. Most people would succeed in small things if they were not troubled with great ambitions."*
>
> —Henry Wadsworth Longfellow

To be sure, there are myriad quotes that both malign and honor ambition in one way or another but Mr. Longfellow quite aptly bolsters our opinion; to whit, one may achieve small things that are great while it is best to leave the great things up to those who are born to accomplish them. Soaring is for eagles, so remember Icarus, who sought to fly too high.

American: There are two types of American: Real Americans and people who think they are American. Real Americans love God, country, mom and apple pie unconditionally. While Real Americans know perfectly well that government is incompetent and despicable, it is nevertheless un-American to question its motives, edicts or policies. Of course, when the government has fallen into the hands of liberals (not Real Americans) then Satan is running loose in the world and it is one's moral duty to complain about everything they do regardless whether it benefits one or not.

Real Americans understand that the rest of the world is insanely jealous of America. They hate Americans because Americans are free and God blesses America.

Real Americans hate the pseudo-Americans and know that the kind of freedoms they cherish should be taken off the books. They want to be able to burn flags, read dirty books and to be able to protest wars and such. And they want to do these things without being watched! Real Americans say if you got nothing to hide then you shouldn't mind a little constant surveillance. Real Americans say, if you can't take the heat, stay out of the kitchen. In other words, "America—love it or leave it!"

Worst of all, un-Americans want to stop Real Americans from exercising their right to stop abortion, pray in schools and carry concealed weapons. It is high time we separate the wheat from the chaff so to speak and clean house of anything even suspiciously un-American!

Amnesty: Something really bad when given to a bunch of illegals just for having squatted in America for a while. Something really good when granted to over zealous freedom fighters from bad countries who have inadvertently killed a few innocents abroad and need to cool their heels in America. Take, for instance, the case of Orlando Bosch, pardoned by GWH Bush and kept away from those evil Cubans who want to try him for blowing up a commercial airliner. Now who wouldn't prefer this ex-patriot to some hard working, honest lowlife from south of the border?

Amnesty International: One of those infuriating NGO's that do a fine job whenever they expose enemies of America as abusers of international rights but can't seem to keep their nose out of the business of friends of America and America itself. Can't these people get it through their heads that America is above the common laws of the world? What America does is ineffable—beyond the comprehension of mere mortal minds! To question is sacrilege!

Amtrak: Zero funding for Amtrak makes a lot of sense because Amtrak is just about trains and who has time to worry about trains? Of course, Amtrak funding also provides for the infra-structure of the rails themselves and it might be a bit of an oversight to let the rails go to hell, especially if we have an emergency like 9/11 and all air flight is cancelled. No matter, by increasing highway funding and allowing Mexican trucking free reign inside America; we don't really need trains anymore.

Anarchy: Anarchy is vastly misunderstood as simply an unordered, leaderless society wherein no rules apply. Anarchists maintain that man does not need an overseer but that each man maintains his own integrity, his moral character and will abide by the golden rule in harmony and friendship with his fellow men. This, of course, is a load of crap invented by people who just can't stand authority. Anarchy is an unworkable social structure except on deserted desert islands.

Anecdotal: Cases or conditions that have a common thread but cannot be used to prove anything are considered to be anecdotal. Citing a single example at a State of the Union Address is not anecdotal but proves conclusively the point intended, usually with heart wrenching poignancy.

Andersen, Arthur: This well meaning accounting firm was convicted of obstructing justice in the Enron scandal for shredding documents pertinent to the case. The Supreme Court, however, overturned the decision on the grounds that there was no compelling evidence that anyone knowingly broke any laws. Apparently, ignorance of the law *is* an excuse!

The media is touting this as a savage blow to the Bush Administration's justice department whose sole *raison d'etre* is to pursue corporate malfeasance, to rout out white-collar criminal behavior and ceaselessly guard the people against powerful interests. (Wink, wink.)

Anger: Anger, considered one of the Seven Deadly Sins is the child of fear. What actually angers us something threatening, something unknown, dark, uncontrolled. Anger transforms fear insofar as we no longer wish to flee but to attack and destroy. Thus, it is quite a useful emotion when properly directed. Keeping the populace angry makes it easy to manipulate. Anger is therefore a virtue, especially when aimed at un-American ideals.

> *"I never work better than when I am inspired by anger. When I am angry I can, write, pray, and preach well; for then my whole temperament is quickened, my understanding sharpened, and all mundane vexations and temptations depart."*
>
> —Martin Luther

Answers, Short and Long: Traditionally, spokesmen, politicians, public relations people, etc. are wont to answer certain questions using the "Short and Long" technique. The Short Answer is usually something like "yes" or "no" and is followed by the Long Answer, which circuitously refutes the Short Answer. Answering in the long is the preferred method. That way one may ramble off into more friendly waters and end up not answering anything at all. Once in a while, however, a stubborn questioner will attempt to recall the original query to which the answerer may either chose to ignore or incredulously exclaim that he or she had just answered it!

Anthrax: Deadly pathogen commonly used to scare the hordes into thinking that America's enemies are poised to dump enormous quantities into our atmosphere by way of cropdusters rented to terrorists or model airplane drones equipped with massive computing and telemetric capabilities. Anthrax is thus a

WMD—Weapon of Massive Distraction. Relax, only the homegrown stuff is really effective.

Anti-Christ, The: You won't know him when you see him until it's too late but at least you know he's going to be a liberal. But being the Anti-Christ, this deceiver will come across as a Conservative because that is the only possible way he will get so many people to follow him.

Anti-Semitism: Hating Jews might have been useful in the past but it's high time we got it together and look for other people to revile. Israel is our good buddy and is a key player in the New American Century so let's just move on. Of course, a little bit of Jew-baiting at the Air Force Academy can be overlooked as just college pranks. And it's not like they're only picking on Jews, so enough with the anti-Semitism.

ANWR: Arctic National Wildlife Reserve—where those dagnabbed caribou keep trespassing on oil rich property. So far the devil worshipping environmentalists have foiled plans to get at that oil but one of these days permission to drill will be tagged onto some "must pass" legislation and then we'll be up to our eyebrows in oil for a few months.

Apartheid: A nasty way of describing any government that creates a whole sub-class of people within its borders. Not to be applied in any way, shape or form to Israel.

Apathy: According to Sir Isaac Newton, a body at rest tends to stay at rest and this is especially true in the case of humans. Apathy in the public domain allows for a minority of active citizens to rule over the passive many. That is just as well since the apathetic many are for the most part the ill-informed, uneducated and unwashed masses.

Aristotle (384–322 BC): One of the granddads of Western Civilization. A no-nonsense, practical sort, Aristotle gave us the black and white of it all, logically speaking. Because of him we can say, "You're either for us or against us", "only one religion can be true" (ours) and all manner of dualistic notions. As a sage, he offered this sage advice to our rulers, "A tyrant must put on the appearance of uncommon devotion to religion. Subjects are less apprehensive of illegal treatment from a ruler whom they consider god-fearing and pious. On the other hand, they do less easily move against him, believing that he has the gods on his side." He may have been a pagan but Aristotle sure knew a thing or two about human nature.

Arms Industry, The: You just can't have enough weapons so there's always work to be done. America is the world's number one arms producer. Without weaponry, the imbalance in trade would be monumental, even though it actually is anyway. Arms dealing is a really good way to give foreign aid because the money just comes right back to America. The Arms Industry—where job security is guaranteed.

Army of One: The new romanticized ideal of the lone soldier able to act out a fantasy of superhuman accomplishment and heroism. Recruits attracted by this advertising gimmick will soon be drummed out of such nonsense. Once inside, the soldier will be shown that teamwork is the essence of success. Every person will look after each other, taking advantage of individual strengths and compensating for weaknesses within the unit without rancor or selfishness. After having loyally served, civilian life will soon drum such nonsense out of every one of them.

Arrogance: The new humility. Effecting a veneer of disdain for others not quite as American as yourself is an act of love; for those you heap it upon will surely wish to emulate the power of your position, thereby becoming more American themselves. Arrogance is tough love, the best kind of love. Empathy or a show of pity toward societal basket cases only reinforces their plight and enables them to continue in their hopeless state. A good show of arrogance is the kind of medicine they both need and deserve. Arrogance toward foreigners lets them know how unlucky they are not to be Americans and gives them the incentive to want to be just like us.

Arthashastra, The: Written circa 400 BC, "the Science of Material Gain" is a text that outstrips Machiavelli in theories of governing a state. It's worth a read for any aspiring tyrant or sage ruler.

Ashcroft, John: President GW Bush's first Attorney General. Ashcroft's brilliant defeat to a corpse in Missouri paved the way for this karaoke krooner and all-around bon vivant to take the spot as America's top cop. Mr. Ashcroft's devoutly religious sensibilities kept him from sitting in judgment of his fellow man, excluding those whom he did not consider to be his fellow man. His most stunning accomplishment as Attorney General was in clothing the bare breasted statues, the *Spirit of Justice* (female) and the *Majesty of Law* (male) within his purview and "repurposing" the Department of Justice in order to combat the greatest impediment to the New American Century, the American people.

Atheist: A high-falutin nincompoop who thinks he and everyone else was an accident of the universe which was itself an accident of who knows what. You won't find any atheists in foxholes because they are all draft dodgers. Nobody who thinks that this is *it* is going to risk it all. Every atheist is a communist or worse with the exception of Ayn Rand. (See Rand, Ayn)

Audacity: The ability to stand up in front of people and claim anything you want is yet another prime attribute of the New American Century politico. White House Press Secretaries need to be audacious as well as scurrilous, long-winded and nimble in their circuitous meandering verbal dances.

Authenticity: The perception of authenticity is what gets Republican votes because the Party is in lockstep over its positions. It doesn't matter what you agree on as long as you stand by it—that shows you are true to your word or cause, that you are authentic. Because there is debate inside the Democrat Party, it means they stand for nothing and are wishy-washy, flip-flopping losers.

Axis of Evil: The so-stated Axis of Evil is the trio of Iraq, Iran and South Korea. One down, two to go. After that there is never a short supply of enemies. Axes apparently come in threes. In World WAR II we had Germany, Italy and Japan. We now have the three noted above. There are three evil enemies of the New American Century: Satan, communism and old-fashioned American patriots.

B is for BI-PARTISAN

Baby Boomers, The: Baby Boomers are those born between 1946 and 1964. Apparently, the Greatest Generation, having exhausted itself on Depression and War turned to sex and created a population boom. Boomers own beat, doo-wap, rock and roll and hippies. Despite all that, look who's leading America today.

Balance of Power: America was set up with a balance of power between the axes of government—the executive, the legislative and the judicial branches—in a kind of rock, paper, scissors sort of arrangement wherein the President appoints judges, cabinet members and other such appointees and has the veto, Congress holds the purse strings and gives the up or down on (some) nominations and the courts decide if either the executive or the legislative are out of bounds. As long as these powers are semi-antagonistic to each other we have gridlock but the New American Century is going to impose a new order on this lousy set up, bringing all three branches in line and on board. When this comes to pass America will be streamlined, in shape and ready to kick ass, no holds barred.

In the past, the so-called Balance of Power was between nations. During the Cold War it was America v. Communist Russia, a.k.a. the Soviet Union lining up face-to-face and toe-to-toe in a drive to see who could out muscle and out missile the other guy. Well, the old USSR has fallen to pieces and the only act in town is America. The whole world is now out of balance and it's up to us to keep it that way.

Bankruptcy: In the New American Century you only get one chance. If you fail you lose. Of course, Corporations that go bankrupt have to be helped by the government, i.e., bailed out by the taxpayers, because, being better than ordinary people, they deserve it. Now, not all corporate bankruptcies necessarily have to rely on the public feeding trough. Some of them have wisely socked away funds for a rainy day in the form of employee pensions. These can be raided and promises broken as easily as an Indian treaty!

Bellicose: A fancy word for loud and obnoxious. Bellicosity is the very best method to use when discussing anything with liberals, communists or any other un-American types. He who is the most shrill and passionate is obviously correct. Responding calmly, logically and cogently to an argument indicates a weak position. Screaming and threatening are the best debate tactics. Bellicosity lends itself well to groups. When two or more overwhelm and shout down the opposition, no dangerous debilitating ideas have the possibility of surfacing. (Compare with Debate)

Beltway, Inside The: A euphemism describing America's go-getters in government service, the punditry, high society insiders and corporate lobbyists. The ragamuffin population within the actual Beltway surrounding Washington, D.C. is definitely **not** Inside The Beltway.

Bible, The: God's science book, history book, manual for living and perennial bestseller. It just goes to show you how crazy a beast is man with all his religions when it clearly says in the Bible that YHWH is God and there is no other. Since that proves it once and for all, every other religion has to be false—including incorrect interpretations of Christianity. When you believe in the Bible in the right way you are accepting things as the Lord made them. Then you know what a measly worm you are and how much you owe Him. It also lets you know what arrogant fools are the unbelievers and how much they actually hate God. Everything they do is to try to make things the way they want them to be in direct opposition to God's will. Why, look at the law—man's law—and see how he tries to keep the Ten Commandments at arm's length! They think that just because we have free will that we should be able to make choices! They think that their abominable lifestyles are natural! They think that man is perfectible and war is not inevitable! They think that there are no rules! That there is no Hell! It's insane! Thank God that God is God and we have His Bible to guide us and His strong arm to comfort us. With God on *our* side we will trample any foe unmercifully, defeat the minions of Satan on earth and conquer all evildoers in our path! Hallelujah! Praise the Lord!

Big Brother: Uncle Sam has passed on the torch to Big Brother in the New American Century. Big Brother is everyone's buddy who's going to keep America safe and secure. Big Brother, like God, is interested in everything you do but unlike God does not have the capability to count every hair on your head—yet.

"The Party seeks power entirely for its own sake. We are not interested in the good of others; we are interested solely in power.... Power is not a means; it is an end...not power over things, but over men.... In our world there will be no emotions except fear, rage, triumph, and self-abasement.... There will be no loyalty, except loyalty toward the Party. There will be no love, except the love of Big Brother.... Always, at every moment, there will be the thrill of victory, the sensation of trampling on an enemy who is helpless. If you want a picture of the future, imagine a boot stamping on a human face forever."

—George Orwell (1903-1950)

Bigotry: A form of tough love with a little unconditional love thrown in. Unconditional because it is bestowed on an entire group without strings or reservation. Tough because it provides a hard lesson to the recipient; namely that their habits and lifestyles are repugnant and they need to clean up their act. Bigotry is wonderful whereas tolerance, acceptance or indifference merely enables and encourages the continuation of horrid behavior.

Big Picture, The: Try as you might you will never see the Big Picture. Therefore, if your opinion runs counter to that of the New American Century you are operating under an incomplete and therefore flawed worldview. That being the case, your opinion is worthless. On the other hand, if you by faith or natural inclination understand that all you have to do is keep your mouth shut, your nose clean and follow orders then there will always be a happy place for you. Just knowing that there are lofty beings that do know the Big Picture and are looking out for your safety moves one toward a peace of mind that passes all understanding.

Bin Laden: There are good Bin Laden's and a bad Bin Laden. Good Bin Laden's are delightful friends of the Bush family. They helped finance the Carlyle Group and are in with the Saudi royalty. The bad Bin Laden is Osama, the black sheep of the family. None of his 50 odd brothers and sisters will have anything to do with him. Nor will his cousins, uncles or close friends.

Bill of Rights, The: That unique appendage to the Constitution of the United States of America that has outlived its usefulness. Indeed, the Bill of Rights is an impediment to the governance of America in the New American Century and it is the duty of every law-abiding legislator to work toward the repeal of these confusing and annoying encumbrances.

Bi-Partisan: Having the Democrats agree to what the Republicans want. Republicans who agree with Democrats are traitors. Of course, as the New American Century progresses, partisanship will become a thing of the past. Those who disagree with the groundswell of popular thought and ideology will be swept aside, cast into the dustbin of history. There will be only one acceptable view. Everyone will know his or her place and disagreement will simply not be tolerated.

Blair, Tony: Current Prime Minister of Great Britain and George Bush's poodle. Blair's help in promoting the Iraq war and "sexing up" the "evidence" against Saddam Hussein will be remembered as long as he is in power. A spot in the Carlyle Group is waiting for him once he's out.

Blame: Wherever and whenever there is conflict, blame must be placed on one side while complete innocence and victimhood is bestowed on the other. For example, the Arabs are obviously totally at fault and full of evil intent while the Israelis are simply trying to live in peace and harmony with their neighbors. Failure to understand this leads to the skewed reasoning that both sides share the burden of responsibility and should make concessions. It also goes against the principle of loyalty, i.e., the notion that one's friends are wonderful and one's enemies are complete scumbags. One does not blame one's friends or family for anything.

Failures in any workings of the New American Century are to be blamed on Clinton. If that is not possible, blame can be attached to any number of false sources. For example, riots in Afghanistan at the Pakistani embassy (due to dissatisfaction with American promises) just happened to occur after Newsweek magazine printed an article about the abuse of the Koran at Gitmo. Obviously, Newsweek caused the riots.

Failures can also be blamed on too many taxes. If the economy is a bit sluggish then it's because there are just too many taxes on the American people in order for them to buy their way out of the doldrums. Naturally, taxes on the rich are especially at fault because everyone knows that rich people spend all their extra cash creating jobs for the little folks so tax relief for the well to do has to be the first order of business.

Blasphemy: Speaking ill of a righteous President who upholds the virtues of the New American Century is blasphemy. Witness Dan Rather's sudden downfall from grace. Maligning Corporations and/or Big Business is blasphemy. So is bad-mouthing Sports, motherhood, guns or pretty much anything about the America way of life. By the way, talking bad about God is also blasphemous but you can always set things right between yourself and your maker.

Blog: Short for Web Log—a site on one of the *Internets* where anyone can keep a personal diary, rant or news journal for all the world to see. Blogging is fast becoming a worldwide craze. Thanks to advanced tracking software, security agencies can quickly add subversive bloggers to lists for future reference.

Blowback: The term for a covert operation that backfires and comes back to bite you. Blowback really has no downside since most of the negative effects occur long after the rewards have been reaped. As well, whatever it is that comes back to bite you must be dealt with and is a kind of long range job security for the spooks, the military and related industries. So Blowback, schmoback. Go for the gusto, let the chips fall where they may and get while the getting's good!

Blue Collar Crime: The perpetration of criminal acts on a lowly scale—to be met with swift and overwhelming retribution. Blue collar crime is to be the media focus far out of all proportions to international political events—except long, drawn out Pope watches, etc. The American people must know that crime is epidemic; that their peers are the perpetrators of said crimes and that the government is being hamstrung by liberal-minded activist judges who mollycoddle these scumbags. (Compare with White Collar Crime)

Blue States, The: The states where the majority of people are confused. (Compare with the Red States)

Board Meetings: Smoky rooms where people discuss how they are going to dominate the world.

Boat People: When coming from Cuba, people who find anything that will float and come to America are "your tired, your poor, your huddled masses yearning to breathe free, The wretched refuse of your teeming shore." America begs, "Send these, the homeless, tempest-tossed to me. I lift my lamp beside the golden door."

When coming from Haiti, they are illegals trying to sneak in uninvited and must be turned back.

Body Armor: American troops are to be outfitted with the semi-best money can buy that does not interfere too much with profits.

Bolton, John: Under Secretary of State for Arms Control and International Security since 2001, Mr. Bolton is currently the Ambassador to the UN, an entity that he hardly recognizes to exist. In keeping with consistency, the President picked Bolton for this highly sensitive diplomatic post because of his lack of sensitivity and diplomacy.

Bombing into the Stone Age: Shock and Awe for any country stupid enough to be set up as an enemy of America. All infrastructures except oil fields, refineries and pipelines are to be obliterated.

Bonaparte, Napoleon (1769–1821): Famed Emperor of France. As dictator, he did not need to be concerned with elections. Nevertheless, he gave this advice to the politician, "If you wish to be a success in the world, promise everything, deliver nothing." As for the ruler, "Never ascribe to malice that which is adequately explained by stupidity." In saying so, he anticipated the Bush Administration.

Born Again: A Christian metaphor for the figurative death to one's sinful past and the figurative rebirth into the family of God. As one may be Born Again but once, it is wise to wait until one sews one's wild oats before taking that final step. Most of our best Christians have done just that and after hitting rock bottom have come to see the light of redemption and self-forgiveness.

Boycott: The willful not buying of a product. Boycotts are insane and should be made illegal and the National Guard should be sent in to break them up!

Brain Drain: While America outsources the more menial jobs overseas it recruits highly skilled and educated foreigners to come and take the only good jobs left. Obviously a win-win situation for Uncle Sam; he gets the best and brightest for cheap while the other country stays in relative scientific and economic poverty. Unfortunately, thanks to No Child Left Behind, the influx of talent into America is kind of a wash since it only replaces the minds lost. But hey, let the other nations foot the bill for education.

Branding: Today, advertising is not so direct. Instead of merely displaying one's product, a company must engage in branding—the linking of some ideal to the company name. Marlboro was years ahead with linking the rugged image of the Marlboro man and the great outdoors to cigarette smoking. The most effective branding links one's company either, as with the Marlboro man, to the rugged outdoors, other manly things, power, prestige or easy sex.

In the old days, branding was what one did to one's livestock. Nowadays, if you can get your girlfriend to tattoo your name on her body then you have in effect branded that filly. A person can also be branded by virtue of an incident in their lives, as in Chappaquiddick Teddy or Hanoi Jane.

Bravado: A necessary trait in New American Century leadership. A good boss is always willing to talk tough and back it up by sending the cannon fodder in to get the job done. Bring it on! (See Bring It On)

Bravery: America is the home of the **brave**. It says so in our national anthem. That being said, the powers that be know perfectly well that America is really loaded up with overstuffed, complacent, apathetic and downright fearful citizens who will go along with just about anything as long as it doesn't inconvenience their daily lives too much.

Bremer, L. Paul: The US Administrator of Iraq, a.k.a. Iraq's sole authority. Bremer is a well-connected insider who, by declaring special decrees and edicts is transforming Iraq into a well-heeled client state and colony of America. Said edicts are posted for anyone to see at http://www.iraqcoalition.org/regulations/ index.html. It's quite a read if you are a masochist. But take a look at Edict 81, #66 which makes it illegal for Iraqi farmers to own their own seed stocks. Quite a coup for Monsanto—and don't think any oil revenues are going to slip through Uncle Sam's fingers. No sirree!

Bring It On: President Bush's manly challenge to all insurgents and foreign fighters to take potshots at Americans in Iraq. It takes a special kind of courage to be able to stand up and sacrifice the troops; a special kind of fortitude to commit the sons and daughters of strangers to harm's way. And you better believe it, George Bush has that special kind of fearlessness that permits him to take up great challenges vicariously. He's spent many a restful night, pillowed by the consequence of his decisions.

Brinkmanship: By definition the practice, especially in international politics, of seeking advantage by creating the impression that one is willing and able to push a highly dangerous situation to the limit rather than concede. In other words, America's foreign policy in the New American Century, for brinkmanship will ensure *nucular* proliferation and guarantee a raft of enemies far into the future.

Buchanan, Pat: Presidential aspirant and famed pundit, Pat Buchanan is an extra-ultra-conservative of the old school with a mishmash of strange ideologies thrown in. Mr. Buchanan, an isolationist, a Catholic and a fierce critic of our porous borders wishes to "take back" America one block at a time with a cadre of armed devotees. He is simply appalled at the New American Century but can be counted on to back the administration to the hilt due to his fear of liberals, Jews, communists and whistle blowing traitors.

Buck, The: An outmoded euphemism for ultimate responsibility as in "The Buck Stops Here." Nowadays, the buck is borne primarily on the backs of the middle class. The buck sails through the Oval Office like a greased pig and is gently distributed over the teeming masses. The greenback, in contrast, is heavily distributed upon campaign contributors, captains of industry, arms merchants and savvy politicians.

Bunker: An underground hideaway where evildoers skulk in safety and luxury while their fellows topside endure horrific fates. Hitler had his bunker and so did Saddam. Americans do not have bunkers. Mr. Cheney owns a fallout shelter. (Compare to Hidey-Holes)

Bureaucrat: Any lefty that worms his or her way into a government post. Bureaucrats exist just to create more bureaucracies, multiplying like vermin and eating at the heart of democracy. That having been said, bureaucracies are somewhat necessary in the business world in order to keep tabs on things. (Antonym: See Public Servant)

Bush, George Herbert Walker (1924–): The 41st and manliest President. This no-wimp tough guy showed his mettle by turning on long time allies Manuel Noriega and Saddam Hussein. Hampered by a powerful Democrat opposition,

Bush nevertheless ushered in a new world order under the guise of a kinder, gentler nation.

As former President, GWH Bush has performed good works in the service of the Reverend Sun Myung Moon, the Bin Laden family and the Carlyle Group.

Bush, George Walker: Dubya, the 43rd President and current War President of America. GW is famous as the clean-up man for the incomplete presidencies of Reagan, Bush (41) and Clinton. As well, he is known for making inventive sayings. An example: "Too many good docs are getting out of the business. Too many OB-GYNs aren't able to practice their...their love with women all across this country." Or: "Tribal *sovereignity* means that; it's sovereign. I mean, you're a—you've been given *sovereignity*, and you're viewed as a sovereign entity. And therefore the relationship between the federal government and tribes is one between sovereign entities." Or: "Our enemies are innovative and resourceful, and so are we. They never stop thinking about new ways to harm our country and our people, and neither do we." Or: "Then you wake up at the high school level and find out that the illiteracy level of our children are appalling." You just gotta love him!

Dubya's hero is Jesus and that's all right—means he's a real man. He's the kind of good buddy you all want to go fishing with and tip a few brewskies. Just send a few hundred thou to the cause and tell him when you'll be in town.

"As democracy is perfected, the office of president represents, more and more closely, the inner soul of the people. On some great and glorious day the plain folks of the land will reach their heart's desire at last and the White House will be adorned by a downright moron."

—H. L. Mencken (1880–1956)

Bush Pioneer: Like a good Pioneer, a Bush Pioneer beats the brush to gather up at least $100,000 for the cause. A Bush Ranger, on the other hand, ranges a bit further and wider to fill the coffers, piling up at least $200,000 to help get GW elected.

Bush, Prescott Sheldon (1895–1972): Father of GWH Bush, Prescott Bush was the first family member in the Skull & Bones and was said to have been in on the theft of Geronimo's skull for the fraternity's safekeeping. PS Bush was a two term Senator following a brief scrape with the law for trading with the enemy during WWII as director of the Union Banking Corp.

Business: The highest endeavor known to man. Business uber alles!

Butler, Smedley, Major General, USMC (1881–1940): This two-time Congressional Medal of Honor winner was actually tapped for the Presidency in a little known coup attempt. But Butler played it straight and went soft as a man of the people. He wrote *War is a Racket*, a little book that's a bit too candid.

C is for CORPORATISM

Caesar, Julius (100–44 BCE): An inspiration to the New American Century. To quote, "When the drums of war have reached a fervor pitch, and the blood boils with hate and the mind is closed, the leader will have no need in seizing the rights of the citizenry. Rather, the citizenry, infused with fear and blinded by patriotism, will offer up all of their rights unto the leader, and do it gladly so." He ought to know, for as he admits in the next line, that's how he did it.

Caesar's downfall was his attempt at land reform. That's why the Senate (the wealthy) rightfully killed him.

CAFE Standards: Standards for fuel efficiency in cars and trucks set by the National Highway Traffic Safety Administration. For light autos, the standard has been frozen at 27.5 miles per gallon since 1990. Apparently, we are at the absolute peak of engine efficiency and cannot improve it at all. Raising the CAFE Standard would be like asking scientists to break the speed of light limit. Too bad—just a few miles per gallon more and we could save so much oil that we wouldn't need to drill in the Arctic National Wildlife Reserve.

Campaign Contributions: Money talks most loudly when funding an election. The laws surrounding campaign contributions are as convoluted as tax law or Senate rules. They are designed that way in order to introduce huge loopholes ripe for exploitation.

Canada: Ordinarily, one tends to ignore Canada as a great big wussy frozen wasteland that is protected by just being next to America but they are beginning to become an annoyance with their cheap pharmaceuticals, especially those man-ufactured in America but sold at a better price north of the border.

Candor: Once in a while a slip of the tongue lets the cat out of the bag. It's better to keep things close to the vest, so to speak, and give the public what it wants to hear rather than being forthright. When asked why they (government officials) repeated things so often, Bush replied, "See, in my line of work you got to keep repeating things over and over and over again for the truth to sink in, to kind of catapult the propaganda." That is a bit too candid for our tastes.

Capitalism: The greatest economic system ever devised by man. Capitalism performs well under any type of government except true democracy unless at least half the population is completely for it.

Carbon Dating: A huge fraud perpetrated by so-called science. Carbon Dating and other fancy-schmancy ways of scientific tomfoolery keep on saying that things are older than the Earth, which is only about 5,000 years old.

Carlyle Group, The: A successful investment group epitomizing the New American Century. Its mission is to "be the premier global private equity firm, leveraging the insight of Carlyle's team of investment professionals to generate extraordinary returns across a range of investment choices, while maintaining our good name and the good name of our investors."
Said investors include many former top American and foreign officials who are able to exploit their connections to maximize profits and effect political pressures to their benefit. In short, a peach of a company.

Carnivore: The last generation of computer software that spies on everyone's emails looking for buzzwords that might lead to suspicious activity. Nowadays, Carnivore is actually defunct—old school. Whatever they've replaced it with has got to be a lot more voracious.

Carter, James Earl, Jr. (1924–): America's 39th President—a mistake of a Democrat who snuck in between Ford and Reagan. Carter's presidency will be remembered for the long gas lines and high inflation rates America suffered under. He also failed at getting America to be energy independent, thus helping to create the mess we're in today.

Caveat Emptor: Old Italian for "Let the buyer beware." Words to live by in the New American Century, as it is high time for product liability laws to be shelved.

Chalabi, Ahmed: We tapped this guy to be our first puppet in Iraq. This expatriated embezzler was definitely our boy, feeding us everything we needed to go into Iraq and then he turned out to be working for the Iranians on the side. It just goes to show that you can't trust even the best of them.

Charity: One of the Seven Heavenly Virtues. It's all right to be charitable but you can't just go around giving things away. That falls into the category of altruism. To be charitable you have to withhold the goods until you get at least a promise that the recipient will clean up his act or you make him pray to get it. Then it's OK to be charitable

Chavez, Hugo: The revolutionary leader of Venezuela and a huge thorn in the side of America. This pipsqueak dictator/elected president is sitting on way too much oil to be taking sides with the poor. Too bad the good people of Venezuela—the rich and well-born—were not able to sustain the failed coup attempt that may or may not have been aided by the CIA.

Recently, our holy friend Pat Robertson has suggested that Chavez should be "taken out." Of course, the left-wing media was appalled and must have great gobs of egg on its face since all he meant that was Chavez should be taken out to a nice dinner and be persuaded to be friendlier to the Bush Administration.

Cheney, Richard: If Karl Rove is Bush's brain, Dick Cheney is his heart. Who manned the COM center during 9/11 while Bush was being spirited here and there? Yes, Dick. Who sat with the President in secret unsworn testimony concerning those trying times? Yes, Dick. Who oversaw secret meetings with energy giants just before the energy "crisis"? Yes, Dick. Who continues to swear that we will find WMD's in Iraq? Yes, Dick. Vice-President Cheney is the can-do and the behind the scenes guy for the New American Century. While millions of Americans saw their savings halved during the first years of the Bush Administration, Cheney cannily managed to triple his net worth, demonstrating that the free market works and works well.

Children, The: One may enact virtually anything as long as one can convince others that it is "for the children". Voting against children is like voting against Patriotism or War and simply is not done except by representatives from liberal hellhole precincts.

Civic Duty: After shopping, the most important duty an American has to his country is to refrain from being poor. The poor don't buy a lot and that's not right. As a moral country we can't just put them to death so poverty is a real problem.

In this age of terrorism, it is also one's patriotic duty to keep a weather eye out for suspicious behavior, especially right in one's own neighborhood.

Lastly, it is every American's duty to obey their leaders in the New American Century.

"Do your duty and leave the rest to Providence."

—Thomas "Stonewall" Jackson

"The very idea of the power and right of the people to establish government presupposes the duty of every individual to obey the established government."

—George Washington

Cheating: Nobody likes a lowdown cheat. But, as it turns out, everybody loves a rascally scamp who bends the rules and takes matters into his own hands for a good cause. Now, that's what it's all about in the New American Century. America is that brash, unconventional scalawag that just isn't gong to knuckle down under the UN or any of those tired treaties made by the old America. You bet that gets America into few scrapes but America will come up smelling like roses and everybody'll just shake their head and laugh. Everybody but the evildoers, of course.

Checks and Balances: In the New American Century, there will be no further need for a government based on checks and balances. A one party system headed up by the POTUS (See POTUS) and backed by a court packed by the POTUS will be much more efficient. Checks and balances will once more become terminology solely associated with banking and bookkeeping.

Chicken Hawk: A supposedly derogatory name applied to pro-war patriots who never had a chance to serve in the military. Consider the source—the lefty draft dodgers! Just because a person had other priorities doesn't mean that they're against war and that's all that counts. Besides, chicken hawks eat chickens!

Child Labor: Thus far, America is lagging behind in this particular category. However, the new testing procedures introduced in the No Child Left Behind program will soon identify those youth who are not fit for academics. Why penalize them when they can become productive members of the labor force? Why subject these innocents to age discrimination? The penal system is accepting children. Why not industry? As they say: if you're old enough to cage, you're old enough for a wage.

Chilling Effect, A: One induces a so-called Chilling Effect on a targeted group by prosecuting one of their numbers to the fullest extent for some minor offense, thus sending a message to the comrades who might have funny ideas to keep in line. Witness the outing of CIA operative Valerie Plame because her husband brought back the wrong info. That will have a chilling effect on any fool who wants to be the bearer of bad news.

Chomsky, Noam: A huge thorn in the side of Imperial America. Chomsky has academic creds up the wazoo and uses his smarts to tell it like it is about American designs on the rest of the world and on its own. As such, he is to be vilified and ignored as much as possible. Fortunately for the New American Century, the corporate controlled media does its level best to keep this guy under wraps.

Choreography: Once solely the province of stage productions and the like, choreography has expanded its horizons into the political and military arenas. No more impromptu town hall meetings where some popinjay might up and ask an embarrassing question. Nowadays, it's essential to script political rallies, frank talks with servicemen and even military operations such as the rescue of Jessica Lynch. It all looks so much more professional this way. And the audience will be so much more appreciative of the well-done production.

Christianity: The only really true religion. Unfortunately, Satan has worked tirelessly to pervert the Truth and has divided Christianity into sects, many of which are as false as any heathen religion and lead only unto damnation. Until the advent of the New American Century, America tolerated some separation of government from religion and where the two intersected there was an inclusiveness that permitted those laboring under misconceived notions to believe that they were represented. "In God We Trust" is a good example. Pretty much all religions believe in a *god*, but clearly, there is only one God and He is the God of the Bible. That having been said, incorrect interpretations of the Bible lead many astray to pray to a false god, for like the Jews, if one does not understand the divinity of Jesus of Nazareth as an integral member of the triune God of the Bible, then one completely misses the picture and is framing in the mind an incorrect idea of Our Father, i.e., an idol. True Christianity demands that one knows to whom one is praying. Fortunately, in the New American Century we have guidelines being provided by the government in the form of its leadership. They have the inside dope. (See the Religious Right)

CIA, The: Formerly used to halt the spread of communism worldwide and foment insurrection in governments America didn't like. Now, to be used in industrial espionage for the sake of American corporations, fomenting insurrection in governments antithetical to the New World Order and maybe intelligence gathering if it is necessary.

Class Action: Class warfare promulgated by a mob bent on stealing money from a corporation because they are jealous of its freedoms.

Class War: The lower classes are to be shamed whenever they engage in the rhetoric of class struggle. They are to be brought up with the notion that America is a classless society, that anyone can get rich and therefore, there's no need to be spouting off about something that does not exist. So in reality, you can't really call it war when one side has been so deluded and stripped of power that they don't even know they're in one.

Clear Skies Initiative, The: Air quality in the New American Century. Unfortunately for our good friends the duck hunters, the skies will be clear of birds.

Clinton, William J. (1946–): As the 42nd President, Bill Clinton, a Democrat, had the effrontery to be a better Republican than his predecessor. His greatest failure was in not even attempting to finish the job abandoned in the previous term, i.e., the colonization of Iraq. Clinton also besmirched the office of the Presidency by getting caught not keeping it in his pants. Although Republicans hate the idea of independent prosecutors, it was necessary to employ the fair and totally nonpartisan Kenneth Starr to spend $40 plus millions in order to get pretty much nothing on Clinton. Other stalwart defenders of righteousness, such as Newt Gingrich also failed to bring Clinton down, themselves imploding in the effort. All in all, the Clinton years will be remembered in infamy as the dark times we faced rising standards in living, peace, security, popularity, good will and prosperity. Thank the Lord that George Bush has reversed these awful trends.

Cluster Bomb: A really keen weapon in America's arsenal. Cluster bombs are like those great fireworks that blow up into a gazillion little pieces and then each of those pieces blows up. Unfortunately, they have a high dud rate and a good percentage of the bomblets don't go off becoming, in effect, highly unstable mines that continually pose a serious threat. Still, Cluster bombs are highly effective in spreading the mayhem and that trumps any associated collateral damage they may cause.

Coalition: Any group of countries that agrees to let America call the shots. If it is necessary to form a coalition for public relations purposes and not enough countries sign on they can be made to change their mind either through bribery or coercion. Either way, they will be willing to sign on. Countries that band together outside of the umbrella of American influence are rogue nations.

Codex Alimentarius Commission, The: Another one of those fun international groups that will have the power to make preventative medicines, herbs and vitamins extremely costly, unavailable and/or profitable to the right parties.

Collateral Damage: Formerly known as the innocent victims of war. Since there is nothing innocent about war, the new terminology is not only appropriate, it sounds more precise and antiseptic in accord with the new smart weaponry and the way we prosecute our conflicts.

Color Code, The: The new Color Code threat level system instituted by the Department of Homeland Security is easily understood and visually appealing. The old color code is as follows: If you're black, get back. If you're brown, get down. If you're white, all right. Both of these codes serve a useful social purpose.

Combat: The exhilarating clash between two mortal foes with all its accompanying sights, sounds and smells—one of man's most thrilling and noble endeavors! Combat may be somewhat tarnished and cheapened by an enemy's cowardice and unwillingness to go mano a machino on the open field against America's superior firepower. Nevertheless, taking video games to the final level is one thrill you won't want to miss!

Communism: The worst type of economic system ever dreamt by man. Communism has to be forced on a populace because it is a totally altruistic system that can only work if everybody goes for it. If everybody did go for it and it didn't have to be forced it would still suck. Man was not meant to share—especially with those of lesser worth, those who don't deserve to be shared with, those who don't work hard, those who don't believe in proper things or anyone at all for that matter. People can give away what's theirs to their hearts content but they should never be forced to part with anything involuntarily. Communism was what caused the fall of man in the first place—when Adam and Eve shared the apple! God disapproves mightily of communism and it is therefore to be shunned, discredited and obliterated.

Compassionate Conservative: After the debacle of the Clinton impeachment, many conservatives were looked upon as mean-spirited and vengeful. Forget all that. While those people have quietly receded, the new Compassionate Conservative has come. He has risen! And now, Conservatives can engage in any sort of activity with a renewed righteousness since they are self-avowedly compassionate.

Competition: As John D. Rockefeller said, "Competition is sin." Collusion amongst the giants of industry and capital is the only way to run a world. However, competition amongst the lower classes is a must in order to keep them occupied and divided, fighting each other for the crumbs of existence. The illusion of competition among the big businesses is a grand deception that both mollifies the great unwashed and encourages them to have at it.

Compound Interest: The Baron de Rothschild exclaimed that compound interest is the eighth wonder of the world! Indeed, it is the proverbial tree upon which money grows.

Compromise: To compromise is just as good as giving in. It's the slippery slope to capitulation!

"From the beginning of our history the country has been afflicted with compromise. It is by compromise that human rights have been abandoned."
     —Charles Sumner (19th century American statesman)

Conflict of Interest: A silly term that is used when one really has a *convergence* of interest in some matter. For example, if a matter of government contracts to a certain company is put before members of Congress who have interests in that company it is said that they have a conflict of interest. Nothing could be further from the truth, for it would seem that these members would have a great deal of interest in all aspects of the situation, especially promoting the welfare of the company. Another example would be if a certain public official in charge of counting votes were also the head of an election committee. Who better to see that their candidate wins?

There is no such thing as a conflict of interest—only a perception of insider dealing, corruption and abuse of power—but those are minor nuisances. In the New American Century, so-called conflicts of interest are to be a criterion for political appointments.

Conscience: A mental affliction that may cause one to regret one's actions. Having a conscience in the New American Century can only prove to be a hindrance.

"It is by the goodness of God that in our country we have those three unspeakably precious things: freedom of speech, freedom of conscience, and the prudence never to practice either of them."

—Mark Twain (1835-1910)

Consciousness: The collective consciousness of Americans is to remain at a low level. Being distracted and kept in a fearful state is the new normalcy. Attaining higher states of consciousness can lead to deep insight and anti-American thought patterns.

Conservative: Conservatism is next to Godliness. It is the philosophy of the upstanding, the virtuous, the free, the brave, the good, the patriotic, the wonderful, the law-abiding, the principled, the loyal, the trustworthy, the stalwart, the resolute, the noble, the family valued and just everything positive you can be that is not enumerated here. Conservatism encompasses everything that is right and good and all other ways of thinking are lowly, immoral, enslaving, untrustworthy, flip-floppity, wavering, ignoble, village-valued and everything negative that you can be that is not enumerated here. Being Conservative is like being Christian—you are right and everybody else is wrong.

Conspiracy Theories: The ravings of paranoiacs. Conspiracy literally means to breathe together. What's so bad about that? Whenever people get together they have to breathe, don't they? Conspiracy fact—now, that's a different story. (See Board Rooms)

Constitution, The: That document that enumerates the laws of the land, to be faithfully followed until it conflicts with doing the right thing for the New American Century. However, in all instances and all occasions the Constitution must be praised to the rafters. When one must move against it or outside it, simply explain that what you are doing was the original intent of the Founding Fathers and you are merely restoring the real and rightful rule of law. As a matter of fact, you can always find one of the first framers who supported the kind of action you want to take. Cite him—or at least paraphrase him.

Consumer Credit: If compound interest is the eighth wonder of the world then consumer credit is the ninth, for it is so deliciously seductive and also pretty much fuels the entire economy of the world. Without the ability to buy now and pay later, consumerism would be nowhere. If people actually had to save up to buy things they would be much more circumspect in their spending. Visa la MasterCard!

Consumerism: The engine that drives the economies of the developed countries of the world. Consumerism is woven into the psyche of modern man—a drive that impels him to go beyond the needs of survival—air, water, food, shelter—and to seek acquisitions for any number of reasons:
Conformity—the need to have what everyone else has.
Ownership—the sheer pleasure of personal control over objects.
Narcissism—pride in one's choices.
Status—establishing one's position through one's acquisitions.
Urge—impulse buying
Mimicry—having those things that one admires has.
Egotism—flouting what one owns.
Rapacity—greed in acquiring.
Insecurity—equating simplicity (having few possessions) with failure.
Satisfaction—the pleasure in buying.
Materialism—the underlying philosophy.
Without the constant cycle of buying, using, trashing, upgrading and pack ratting the world would fall back into barbarous decay. Imagine a world bereft of hot dog cookers, chi-chi balls, designer cell phone covers, fruit shaped kitchen magnets...it's too hideous to contemplate. If there exists any kind of evolution in this world it is the evolution of man from hunter/gatherer to wanter/gatherer. As the saying goes, "He who dies with the most toys wins."

Consumer Protection: A nonsensical notion put forward by business hating communists. Every consumer is protected by the ultimate freedom of either buying something or not buying it. If someone buys something then they have waived any right to some ethereal notion of being 100% certain they bought what they paid for. (See Caveat Emptor)

Contempt: Contempt is a feeling one should have for liberals and the like. As for our leadership, Contempt for others is a natural state of existence. Obviously, one must have Contempt for the "have-nots", for their use in society is limited to only the raw labor they produce. They are the great unwashed whose lives totally lack any meaning. One certainly has Contempt for any opposition to the Upper Classes for these people would attempt to create a world that is not a zero sum game, where wealth would be distributed more equitably. That is a sin against everything and deserves not only Contempt but annihilation as well. Finally, one must have Contempt for the underclasses that serve, for they are either obsequious toadies, oblivious fools or are content to be ground underfoot out of a misguided sense of security.

Context: To quote, paraphrase, etc. out of context is the only way to communicate what one has to say rather than what the original source intended. To quote in context is to inform, to elucidate and takes a lot of time and care—therefore, today's media rightfully avoids it.

Kudos to Fox's Brit Hume for totally misrepresenting FDR's statements concerning social security by taking parts completely out of context. Mr. Hume used various snippets and put together a case that went exactly opposite of FDR's sentiments and coincided precisely with the Bush Administration's ideas of reform.

Contraception: The willful killing of pre-babies—right up there in sinfulness with masturbation.

Contracts, No-Bid: Government contracts awarded to companies that are perfectly suited for the job at hand and therefore, no competitive bidding for said contracts is necessary. The ultimate criteria for obtaining no-bid contracts are determined by previous campaign contributions and generous kickbacks.

Contracts, Cost-Plus: A way to sweeten the pot for any company on the public dole. Cost-plus simply means you can add on all kinds of extravagant expenses and the taxpayers have to cough up the cash. Halliburton is paving the way to a New American Century by taking full advantage of no bid, cost-plus contracts in Iraq, thus removing available funds from the coffers of spendthrift liberals who would waste it on the poor.

Contract Workers: People with useful skills in America's efforts at nation build-ing. A Contract Worker may also be a mercenary—a person skilled in warfare and not encumbered by military protocols or restrictions. Contract workers make up the second largest force in Iraq.

Conventional Wisdom: Conventional Wisdom is anything that you wish every-one to believe. For example, it is universally accepted that a single payer insurance plan for America simply will not work. (Not because we've tried it and it failed but because it is not in the best interest of the insurance companies.) And so, that is that as far as that goes!

All sorts of things go unchallenged because they have been ingrained into the psyche of the American belief system. It matters not whether these things are the "best" or even if they make sense. What matters for the future is that the root of Conventional Wisdom stems from the tenets of the New American Century.

Corporations: God's gift to mankind. Only God can create life but He has blessed men with the ability to create *people* (thus assuaging vaginal envy) in the form of Corporations, for Corporations are indeed legally people who are far superior to man in every respect. Corporations are naturally endowed with the Spirit of Americanism and are not restrained by conscience, morality or loyalty. They are the highest form of personhood and as such, deserve every consideration and protection against those who would file frivolous claims against their well being and the welfare of their shareholders.

Corporatism: The much-maligned Benito Mussolini aptly described Fascism as Corporatism. Alas, so many nasty associations are drawn where there should be none. After all, Fascism was named after the Latin "fasces"—a bundle of sticks bound together. So what's the harm in a bundle of sticks?

Since corporations are superior to men it is only fitting that corporations should take a role in leading that man-made mess called government.

Corruption: Using one's power and/or position for personal gain is not corrupt as long as it is in the best interests of the New American Century. Consider the meaning of the word itself. Corruption connotes decay, as in the corruption of a corpse rotting in a dank tomb. Such an image is totally at odds with streamlining American government with modernity and efficiency through the corporate model with all its slick branding, high gloss and sexy appearance! Uncle Sam has got a laptop and a cell phone plugged into today's hip society. He's a shark who's taking names, kicking ass and making the folks he's screwing foot the bill.

Coup d'etat: OK, so there's a French word that's useful. Helping a country overthrow its leaders without having to get our hands dirty is a fine old American tradition. Once in a while a coup goes bad but you can't win them all. The coup attempt in Venezuela to get rid of that pesky Hugo Chavez was so close you could taste it! Then at the last hour a few "patriots" came to rescue the constitutionally elected leader and restored him to power. @#$#%&$!

Coulter, Ann: Equine-faced goddess of sanity and wit in the New American Century—authoress and journalist whose no-holds-barred critique of liberalism is matched only by her complete lack of scruples, references and source data. In the past, her commentary was especially spicy due to her uncontrollable unrequited lust for Bill Clinton—played out with all the fury of a woman scorned.

On Islamic countries: "We should invade their countries, kill their leaders and convert them to Christianity. We weren't punctilious about locating and punishing only Hitler and his top officers. We carpet-bombed German cities; we killed civilians. That's war. And this is war."

On liberals: "When contemplating college liberals, you really regret once again that John Walker is not getting the death penalty. We need to execute people like John Walker in order to physically intimidate liberals, by making them realize that they can be killed, too. Otherwise, they will turn out to be outright traitors."

Her Biblical interpretation: "God says, 'Earth is yours. Take it. Rape it. It's yours.'" What a woman!

Courage: Courage is a French word. America is the home of the **brave** and has no room for the courageous. You can have Fortitude, too, because that's a fancy word for being brave and it's another one of those Seven Heavenly Virtues.

Courts, The: Like the media, the courts are packed with flower sniffing, fruity liberals and that's why we have to have automatic sentencing to ensure criminals get what they deserve. Until good-hearted Conservative judges are packed into the courts we will be at the mercy of street crime, terrorists and evildoers of every stripe. A strong judicial system goes hand in hand with a strong penal system and that's a family value no one can deny.

Covenant Marriage: The new craze legal in all of three states that uses superglue to bind a marriage contract. Now the sacred pact has two options, regular or covenant, the low and high-octane versions of that old family tie. Divorcing from a Covenant Marriage is about as easy as getting an abortion from Dr. Dobson.

Cover-Up: The knee-jerk reaction of anybody trying to avoid taking responsibility for a failure or a crime. Cover-ups usually bring more rebuke than the original act, for people can be quite forgiving if one simply confesses and repents. Cover-ups are unnecessary in the New American Century because if a law is broken it will be a simple matter to change the law and grant pardons retroactively.

Creation Science: From God's science book comes the official version of the great beginning of everything.

Credibility: America has all the credibility in the world. From now on, if America says it's so then every other nation knows that that's the way it's going to be!

Critical Thinking: A harmful and seditious practice. Critical thinking is being stamped out by education in the New American Century and is being replaced by strategic test taking skills. A typical example would be filling in the blank in a given relationship as in, Mainstream Media is to George W. Bush as "blank" is to William J. Clinton. Answer: Monica Lewinsky.

All of the methods for creating and maintaining a desired society have been worked out in the past and therefore, this once useful mental procedure has become counter-productive. America is willing to outsource critical thinking if required but far-flung planning and well thought strategy are simply unnecessary. When you hold all the cards, what can go wrong?

Criticism: Justified when applied to liberal monkey business. Otherwise, criticism is hurtful and can lead one to be audited by the IRS.

Cronyism: A harsh term used by jealous outsiders attempting to deride the business world and government about how they work.

Crusade: A misunderstood term used to describe how we are going to bring freedom, liberty and justice to the Muslim world.

Cult: Any so-called religion that is not of the Judeo-Christian persuasion. Unfortunately, there are many cults that claim to be Christian. The only way to be really sure is to get a feel for the kind of sect that Billy Graham would find passable. Catholics are in a really gray area. Mormons, while we love you and know you've got the right mind politically, we're afraid you completely miss the boat with your wacky religion.

Culture: They say that because America is such a melting pot that it really doesn't have a culture. That's not true but to define American culture isn't that easy. The best way to describe it is to say what it isn't. It isn't Mexican, Canadian, British, certainly not French or any kind of European, South American, African, Asian or Australian.

There are some things uniquely made in America but our minorities usually create them. Sooner or later, white folks take them up and make them presentable (like Pat Boone cover records of Little Richard hits), thus keeping our minorities on their toes, culturally speaking, to uncover new forms of art and entertainment. Now jazz is great, rock 'n' roll is all right (even though it leads to licentious behavior) but this gangsta rap is a bit problematic. As long as white kids go for the good rap then it's OK if not a bit mystifying.

Culture of Life, The: The name given to those followers of the correct way to understand Christianity with respect to the unborn and the persistently vegetative. These God fearing defenders of the innocent are true believers in the New American Century and someday, the whole wide world will be shown the light. Proponents of the Culture of Life generally support war, the death penalty for the mentally disabled and obsess upon their own death as the gateway to salvation.

Czar: Czar is Russian for king. It's also sometimes presented as tsar, but Czar looks and sounds a lot tougher and that's the idea because in America we want to be tough on drugs. So we have a Drug Czar—a tough guy who has zero tolerance for evildoers and lawbreakers. Who's our current Drug Czar? Who cares? We're in a war on terrorism right now and we don't have time for sideline action.

D is for DEMOCRACY

Daily Show, The: The fact that most Americans from 18–49 prefer this fake news show hosted by John Stewart and his wacky gang of faux journalists speaks volumes about the so-called real news. That people prefer a program that follows a show about puppets making crank phone calls is indicative of how much respect the pundits deserve.

Stewart is an equal opportunity offender but it seems like he finds a little too much to spoof about the Republicans and the Bush Administration. And worst of all, he sports a segment entitled "This Week in God" which ridicules religions. Now, we've already come to the conclusion that all the fake religions are silly but Stewart and his man, Rob Corddry play it a little fast and loose with Christianity as well. That is over the top!

DARE: **D**rug **A**buse **R**esistance **E**ducation. Like Abstinence Only education, a publicly sponsored program designed to make sure that a good number of children will do the opposite of its ostensibly intended purpose. By creating outrageous myths about drugs, DARE agents induce a high level of inquisitiveness in America's youth, thus ensuring the continuation of the Drug War and the Prison Industrial Complex.

Darwin, Charles (1809–1882): Demonic founder of the "religion" of Evolution—that unholy attempt to discredit the Bible and make a mockery of God's plan. Scientists continually try to revise and rework Evolution Theory in order for it to make sense but it can never answer all of the questions. The obvious answer—God did it—is right under their backsliding, atheistic noses but they refuse to smell the roses.

Death Penalty, The: We must keep death alive! Any country that goes soft on the death penalty is likely to go soft on war. America is Pro-Life and pro death penalty because it cares. Simpering, criminal pampering liberals are Anti-Life and anti-death penalty because they are conflicted, misguided, confused and weak. Currently, there is a resurgence of anti-death penalty fanatics simply because it has come to light that minorities are sentenced to death more often than whites and that many people on death row are actually innocent of the crime for which they are sentenced. Boo hoo! It's not like Americans aren't willing to hang ninety-nine innocents in order to make sure they got the guilty one. Besides, they must be guilty of something.

Death Tax, The: Formerly known as the Estate Tax, now a.k.a. as the Paris Hilton Tax. This tax must be abolished because it punishes the wealthiest in our society just for being born! Repeal of the death tax will not affect 98% of the population except that they will be proud to understand that America does not discriminate against her rich.

The Founding Fathers foolishly insisted upon an Estate Tax in order to prevent certain families from becoming dynasties. America needs dynasties because it's the richest class of folks that keep getting elected. And they're the one's who have the time to do public service anyway. Poor people are too busy trying to scrape a living than to be running for office. They don't grow up able to see the Big Picture so their brand of politics is silly anyway.

Debacle: The new word for disaster when pertaining to failed policies of the New American Century. Using the word debacle takes the sting out of the situation because it is an odd word that can be mispronounced in funny ways.

Debate: An exchange of opposing ideas. Ideas that oppose the tenets of the New American Century are ludicrous and are not worthy of debate, even as intellectual exercises. Nonetheless, there are crafty dissidents and naysayers afoot and one must always be on the ready to refute any and all contrary arguments. A zinging response to an argument against anything American would be, "If you don't like it so much, why don't you just move to China and be with your buddies?" Or just give them a good old civilized thumping.

Debt: America's in debt. We had a $5 trillion reserve just sitting there doing no good but now we've invaded Iraq and have a War of Terror to prosecute. That has put us about $7 trillion in the hole. But hey! The government should run its business like you run your household. Aren't you mortgaged to the hilt? Think of it. You owe all kinds of money, don't you? Well, America owes, too and that's as American as apple pie!

Decency: Decent behavior in the New American Century is concerned with the way one comports oneself in language and in sexual matters. A decent person does not swear (publicly), nor does he or she engage in illicit sex (publicly—that is, does not get caught). Doing right by others was once considered decent behavior. That is fine for the throng but it is hardly profitable.

Defense: Protecting military, governmental and corporate assets worldwide. Saving the lives of the citizenry is an added plus—called a collateral benefit. (Compare to National Security)

DeLay, Tom: Former House Majority Whip, Tom "The Hammer" DeLay is not one to let the law get in his way to get his way. Thrice admonished by the House ethics committee for unseemly practices, DeLay had the House rules changed so that he could remain in power while under investigation for several alleged violations. Such dealings are helping to push the bubble on promoting the New American Century, especially toward one party rule with its ability to change laws as fast as they break them.

Mr. DeLay is currently under investigation for some of his fine dealings. Of course, those who seek to tear him down are members of the vast liberal conspiracy that would just love to see America fail because they hate America and great Americans like our Majority Whip. Well, Ton DeLay was once a big time exterminator in Texas and we're all hoping that he will crush these creeps like bugs in a blanket.

While not an original PNAC (Project for a New American Century) member, as a premier member of the Culture of Life, Delay is way on board as far as our foreign policy goes. He said without equivocation, "In short, it is the position of the people of the United States, as expressed by their representatives in Congress, that Israel's fight is our fight. And so shall it be until the last terrorist on earth is in a cell or a cemetery."

DeLay is right in line on many a major issue. For example, on the environment: "The EPA, the Gestapo of government, pure and simply has been one of the major claw-hooks that the government maintains on the backs of our constituents."

Mr. DeLay is one of the most successful donation hounds in all of American history. His war chest has sponsored many a Republican campaigm, allowing him to become a powerful influence peddler amongst his peers. For this reason the wagons have thus far encircled him in his moment of trial but as the flames get a little closer, the loyalty of those beholden to him will be tested to the limits.

Democracy: A really atrocious political philosophy which thankfully has never been tried in America. Democracy is, after all, mob rule, the tyranny of the majority (which is mostly poor white trash and all kinds of ethnic types). One shudders to think! However, no one seems to understand that America is an Oligarchy but believing that it is a democracy mollifies the populace. Moreover, it has become quite trendy to invade other countries under the guise of spreading democracy around the world. Somehow, the idea of giving people the right to vote for a puppet has been thrown into the mix and so a few well-orchestrated elections have sufficed to further the charade.

Democrat Party, The: No longer a useful appendage as the "loyal opposition". Opposition, like competition is sin. The New American Century requires a one-party system in order to grease the skids of deregulation, eliminate unfair taxation of the wealthy and remove impediments to empire. Besides, since many of the Democrats are falling all over themselves to become Republican-Lites, why don't they just join up like their good old buddies from the South did?

Demonize: The practice of character assassination—exaggerating the faults of another to an extraordinary degree. Liberals often accuse conservatives of demonizing them and their doings but to what end would it be to demonize the demonic? They, however, know no shame when uncovering a foible or two. They rant and rave and create tempests in a teapot. They like nothing better than to persecute the righteous and tilt at the windmills of the New World Order.

Denial: An auto-response of the human nervous system particularly heightened in public officials. Denial is useful in that the people simply cannot believe what is being done to them and will go on as if nothing is happening.

Depleted Uranium: A wonder of the modern world! DU is not only an excellent addition to our weaponry but it also helps to solve our problems with spent fuel rods by scattering them all over creation rather than having to bear the cost of burying the stuff. That's the reason we fight them over there so we don't have to fight them at home—we wouldn't want to trash America with stuff that has a half-life of 4.5 billion years!

Deregulation: The removing of those nasty obstacles to profits. Once deregulation has run its course in a particular industry (all the profits have been sucked out and the industry is in shambles), it is then necessary for the taxpayers to clean up the mess and start the regulation/deregulation cycle all over again.

Details : Often bothersome little parts of a picture. It is said that the Devil is in the Details. Hence, details must be culled so as to remove the Devil and present a proper perspective. For example, the Details of the Joseph Wilson trip to Africa are:

1. CIA chiefs request an evaluation of the credentials of Joseph Wilson from his wife, Valerie Plame, now working a desk after having been an undercover agent.

2. Ms. Plame provides her husband's bona fides.

3. Mr. Wilson goes to Africa, returns and reports that there was no attempt by Saddam Hussein to obtain yellow cake uranium.

None of the above Details were known to the American people and were rightly ignored (especially #3) by the Bush Administration in its lead up to the invasion of Iraq. However, Mr. Wilson went and blabbed and his wife was subsequently (consequently?) outed as a CIA operative, a move which seems to have backfired on the Administration. Now, in order to discredit both husband and wife, Ms. Plame has been accused of nepotism in hiring her husband to go to Africa. This required ignoring Detail #1—and the fact that Valerie Plame had no personal authority to hire anyone for any mission.

Alas! All the Details have managed to come out and it looks like the Administration is having a devil of a time trying to continue to ignore them.

Détente: Back in the hottest days of the Cold War we used détente to ease tensions between America and the Russkies. Now that that's over, we don't have to use any fancy froggy words for anything. Détente means, "a relaxing" and the only relaxing we're going to do is in a Kuwaiti health spa while the frenchies beg us to let them in. No way, René.

Development: As related to 3rd world countries, development consists of massive loans to be repaid by allowing multinational corporations complete access and dominion over all natural resources.

Dictatorship: A desirable form of government in that there are no hindrances to the implementation of policy—just so long as the dictator is an ally to America and believes in the New American Century. Dictators who do not ally themselves with America are awful, rapacious evildoers. Dictators that do ally themselves with America had better watch their back and take a lesson from Marcos, Noriega, Saddam et al.

Diebold: One of the premier companies of the New American Century. Diebold's paperless voting machines will end all possibility of voter fraud by liberals.

Digress: To digress is to stray from the subject at hand. A good spokesman will segué into softer territory whenever a difficult question has been posed.

Kudos to the punditry for its massive digression concerning the recent scandalous Downing Street memo that implicates our beloved President in faking the reasons for going to war with Iraq. As it happened, W. Mark Felt, formerly the #2 man at the FBI during the Nixon era revealed himself to be "Deep Throat." This revelation allowed the press to make some quick comparisons and points of demarcation between the actions of Mr. Bush and Mr. Nixon and then to segué into a fierce debate over whether Mr. Felt is a traitor or a hero. Along the way the American people have forgotten the Downing Street memo as well as the crimes perpetrated by former President Nixon and his staff. Again, kudos to the press for deftness and aplomb!

Diplomacy: The strategy of losers, those in a one-down position, of those who don't have the muscle or the nerve to go for the brass ring. Teddy Roosevelt did say, "Speak softly but carry a big stick," in which case, one may pretend to be diplomatic and soft spoken but in the long run all parties involved know the true score.

Diplomats: Members of the idle rich who hob-nob around the world, partying and rubbing elbows with foreign potentates on the government's dime. Diplomats are a way of countries adding the human touch to communications.

Dissident: An un-American scumbag that opposes the inevitability and righteousness of the New American Century. Dissidents are flag burning, rabble rousing, communist loving baby killers.

Dittohead: A good citizen who relegates his thinking to Rush Limbaugh in order to free up time for better things such as shopping and tailgate parties.

Diversion: Any hot topic that inflames the public and consumes their attention while the good work of empire building, fleecing the yokels and/or consolidating domestic control goes unnoticed. Diversions in general have little or no effect on the working of the economy. There are two types of diversion—natural and manufactured. Natural diversions occur as a matter of course. Examples of this type are celebrity weddings and divorces, natural disasters, sensational trials and the perennial diversion, sports. A few excellent examples of manufactured diversions are flag burning, school prayer, the death penalty, abortion and timely political exposures. "Must pass" legislation is inherently diversionary as lawmakers may insert all sorts of pork or draconian laws with virtual impunity.

Diversity: Diversity in the New American Century is employing women and minorities that agree with the status quo in order to trump the crybabies who feel they're being kept from getting in on the action. As well, trotting out an archconservative minority serves the dual purpose of recruiting voters from that minority and demonstrating how accommodating conservatives really are.

The old idea was to "level the playing field"—an outrageous idea—and make sure that everyone was represented in the workplace and in government service. This lead to the practice of quotas and reverse discrimination, enraging white trash and getting out the conservative vote.

DLC, The: The Democrat Leadership Council—the heart of the Republican-Lites. A.k.a. as DINO's—Democrats In Name Only—these guys are totally confused as to whom they owe allegiance. Nevertheless, they are useful inasmuch as they rubber stamp Republican nominees and legislation. One supposes if there is such a thing as a good Democrat this is where to find one. (See Useful Idiots)

Dobson, Dr. James: Doctor of Philosophy, prolific author of parenting guides and founder of *Focus on the Family*, Dr. Dobson is one of the central figures in today's effort to put God back into the political scene. According to Dobson, virtually every facet of mainstream secular society is a direct attack upon religion and in particular, fundamental Christianity. Coming from this angle, it would appear that religious persecution is not only on the rise but is entrenched in American society to the degree that even cartoon characters continually assault young minds in an attempt to pervert them. Never fear. Dr. Dobson and his considerable following are tirelessly combating the rising tide of humanism. At every turn they thwart evil. Step by step they endure the relentless barrage, armed with righteousness and divine purpose. They will never waver. Nor will they cower. Truly, they will inherit the earth!

As it stands, Dobson dovetails nicely with the tenets of the New American Century and is a powerful ally in the cause. Unfortunately, he knows this and is evermore beginning to assert his influence, demanding payment for his allegiance in the form of judicial nominees and the forwarding of problematic legislation. Not that his demands are too bothersome—it's just a matter of timing and public perception. Moving too fast and seeming to be unduly influenced by the religious right will arouse the ire of the real silent majority, the apathetic mob.

Docility: A desired trait in the population with the exception of those intended for the armed services, police or prison work and professional sports.

Domestic Consumption: That which is appropriate to American ideals. Unfiltered news reports, opinions and editorials are not for Domestic Consumption.

Dominionism: Our friends in the "Biblical Christianity" movement insist that everything is secondary to the second coming of Christ wherein this mess of a world—having given dominion over to Satan since the fall of man—is going to have its act cleaned up. That is, the teachings of Jerry Falwell, et al. are the right and true way to run everything and so this way of life has dominion over all others. OK, so long as nothing runs counter to the New American Century.

Don't Ask, Don't Tell: America's military is not on a witch-hunt to find homosexuals amongst its ranks. It merely suggests that gays should remain closeted and discreet. That way everyone can pretend that like atheists, there are no queers in foxholes.

Double Standard: Since there are two classes of people—the wealthy and powerful and the not wealthy and not powerful—there are two sets of ways to deal with each class. For example, if a poor person is caught with a minute amount of crack cocaine then he must go to jail for a predetermined inordinate amount of time whereas if an executive is found to have been using the same substance he must go to rehab—or not.

Dove: Slang for a lily-livered, anti-American peacenik. Named after the wussy little bird. (Contrast with Hawk)

Downing Street Minutes, The: This so-called "smoking gun" minutes that alleges that the Bush Administration had secretly planned to invade Iraq as early as 2002 and wanted to fake the evidence against Saddam Hussein in order to convince the people that it was necessary to effect said invasion is totally without merit since it is clear that America (and the Brits and the whole world of the willing) took out the Iraqi leadership in order to free the Iraqi people of this evil Hitlerian dictator as well as end the corrupt Food for Oil Program that also enslaved them. Since Saddam obviously had no weapons of mass destruction and was no threat to his neighbors can any sane person believe that this was the reason for invading? Of course not! One doesn't invade another country on the grounds that the absence of proof is not the proof of absence! So, do these people who allege misdoings believe that the world would be better off with Saddam in power—a Saddam who obviously *wanted* weapons of mass destruction in order to create havoc and menace the entire globe? And don't forget the rape rooms, his insane sons, ties to terrorism and his unwillingness to pay us to build pipelines at our prices.

Draft, The: There is an ongoing myth that the Draft will soon be reinstated. This is absolute nonsense but having said that, the idea is on the table. Presently, there is an ample pool from which to obtain troops. (1) Volunteers—technically speaking, since America has an all-volunteer military, they're all volunteers but there are volunteers and there are volunteers. The number one choice of any military is the gung-ho, everyone in the family served, tell me where to sign and what to do, red-blooded all-American boy (or girl). (2) Stop Loss—Already there, already trained (you didn't read the fine print) troops account for a goodly number. (3) Reserves—trained weekend warriors whose time has come to pay the piper. (4) Recruits—Thanks to No Child Left Behind we have an aggressive high school recruitment program. If we can't convince them to join out of patriotic duty we sell the glitz, glamour and glory of military service or reveal the raw fact that it's the only job they're qualified for (remember all those late night video games when you should have been doing your homework) or are likely to get. (5) Aliens—promising scrappy young foreigners the fast track to American citizenship makes for a diverse military. (6) Mercenaries—heavily armed contract workers. Unfortunately, despite all these resources, America is falling short on its ability to get people to volunteer. But, we do have one last resort—robots! (See Drones)

Draft Dodger: A low down varmint too scared to put on a uniform. It's one thing if you are somebody and have good reasons for a deferment but anybody else who runs from the call ought to be shot.

Drones: American technology is enabling us to send robots to war. We are already sending surveillance drones loaded with munitions to not only find our enemies but to blow them to smithereens as well. And these kamikazes don't flinch!

Drugs: There are good drugs and there are great drugs. Good drugs are made by pharmaceuticals and have unfortunate side effects that tend to kill about 100,000 Americans every year. That's a shame but there's a lot of money to be made in the pharmaceutical business, especially in psychiatric drugs for kids. Great drugs are illegal and there's a TON of money to be made in the War on Drugs on both sides of the picture.

Drug War, The: A divinely inspired way in which to make money and prisoners. Of course, if businessmen, beloved pundits or the sons and daughters of the wealthy are found to be involved with drugs then it is a medical concern and kept clear of the penal system. For the riff-raff, however, it's going to be long manda-tory sentences and property seizures to send the message rippling through the ether that America has no tolerance for hanky-panky with unregulated mood altering substances. (See Double Standard)

Duct Tape: America's first line of defense—one of the items necessary for sur-vival in the New American Century. Along with plastic film, duct tape will repel biological and chemical attacks. Your leaders, especially those with business ties to home maintenance centers want you to know that while they are hunkered and bunkered they want the American people to be as fully equipped as our battle ready troops.

In case of *nucular* attack, either crouch under a desk or lie in a ditch and cover with a door. Hopefully there will be a door near the ditch you are in.

Dueling: Fighting to the death over a matter of honor is currently outlawed in America. However, the right to carry concealed weapons even into barrooms is working its way through various state legislatures in an apparent hope to revive this old and time-honored institution.

Dumming Down: The ultimate goal of public education and the mainstream media is to ensure that the populace is reduced in the capacity to reason and therefore cannot understand what exactly is being done to them. As there will always be those who rise above expectations, these few individuals must be either culled from the crowd for private instruction or medicated into mediocrity according to their predilections.

In the past it was necessary to allow for a self reliant and competent population in order to tame the wild reaches but now that we have secured the boundaries, an intelligent throng will only get itself into mischief. Imagine a land of philosopher custodians, scholarly soldiers or learned factory drudges! Unworkable! Today's society must fit the bell curve, ensuring uniformity, continuity and predictability to its political, military and industrial leadership.

E is for EMPIRE

Economics: The economic theory of the New American Century can best be described as Reaganomics on steroids.

Economic Growth: A condition that must persist forever or the consequences are so dire as to be unmentionable. Fortunately, since one tends to tie the Economy to sales and since there is continued population growth—hence more sales—it appears that growth is simply a natural phenomenon. Nevertheless, growth must be attributed to one's political policy in order to gain favor in the sight of the mob.

Economic Indicators: A mish-mash of contributing factors that may be quantified to give an overall picture of the health of the Economy. Since economics is clearly incomprehensible, it is a matter of course to select various indicators and arbitrarily assign to them worth (impact upon the Economy) in order to present the public with the desired picture.

Economic Policy: America's economic policy has and always has been to ensure the stability and prosperity of her wealthy class while bestowing the liberties of the free market system upon the populace—that is, imposing austerity programs upon the middle class. It matters little how this is accomplished—merely that those in charge of the economy must explain the intricacies of their craft with enough apparent sincerity to, if not appease the great masses, then to at least keep their grumbling down to a minimum. One tried and true tactic is to simply maintain at all times that the economy is great and getting greater every day. Plunges in the market, massive lay-offs or soaring prices can be readily explained as "adjustments", the free market having the ability to "settle" itself into more stable positions.

Economy, The: A chaotic system of smoke and mirrors that no one can predict or understand. When things seem good then the Economy is doing well. If things are bad then one must "tweak" the system in hopes of forestalling an economic crash.

Education: Education is not a birthright. It is a privilege and is the national day-care system for children until they are 17 or so. Since this is a great burden on the American taxpayer, education also must provide each child with enough smarts to get a job, join the military or end up in jail. (Contrast with Home Schooling)

Ein Volk, ein Reich, ein Fuhrer: One people, one empire, one leader. Catchy little phrase, that. Hitler had it easy because the Germans were overwhelmingly one people. The New American Century needs a slogan like this but because America has become such a mutt hole of a country it's pretty much impossible to consider it as one people.

Eisenhower, Dwight David "Ike" (1890–1969): Our 34th President and the Supreme Allied Commander of the Armed Forces in WWII. In a candid moment, Eisenhower warned us of the dangers of a military-industrial complex. Fortunately, that was during his farewell speech so he couldn't do anything about it. (See Appendix D)

Elections: Events staged every so often designed to impress an opinion upon the rabble. In an "open and free" election, the people are led to believe that their opinion counts. In openly controlled or corrupted elections, the people have no illusions toward controlling their own destinies. It is up to the ruling elite to decide what impression they wish to make. (See Voting)

Electoral College, The: The last defense of the ruling elite against voting by the common herd. Even though the Founding Fathers capitulated to the Amendment process, they made damn sure to get this one right.

Embedded Reporter: Any member of the 4th Estate that has the OK to hang with the troops as long as he keeps sending in the positives of war and occupation. What unarmed civilian in his right mind would send home blaring exposes and harsh criticisms of those who are protecting his life?

Emotion: In the New American Century appeals to reason are to be avoided at all costs. What is necessary in order to sway the mob is to couch all arguments in emotional terms. That way, any debate will be qualified with emotional sound bites, thus heading counter arguments off at the pass. For example, the intended policy of privatizing social security accounts—said policy having no bearing on shoring up the trust fund—must be prefaced with the claim that "we must save social security!" All subsequent arguments pro and con will thus be framed within the notion that social security must be saved, virtually guaranteeing that whatever is ultimately done can be enshrined in the nobility of that purpose.

Empire: Of old, empires were countries that held other countries as colonies. Today, the only empire is America but it does not hold other countries as out-right colonies (with a few exceptions). Rather, the American empire allows any country to have its own government and *sovereignity* as long as it remains loyal to America, adheres to the tenets of the New American Century, is docile, subjugates its citizens and subjects itself to the IMF and World Bank.

Ends, The: That which always justifies the means.

Energy Task Force, The: Headed up by Vice-President Cheney right after being sworn in. Who attended these meetings concerning America's energy policy is a secret thanks to executive privilege. What the meetings were about, however, is well known; namely, getting together a bunch of energy brokers (such as Enron) and gouging the citizens of that abominable blue state, California.

Enron: A naughty, naughty company. While one has to applaud their daring, initiative and inventive business practices, when they got caught and didn't have a well-placed scapegoat at hand it put a lot of heat on the business community at large. Big business works best when its dealings are kept private and any company that calls attention to the nuts and bolts has gone beyond the pale.

Entitlements: The deviants and miscreants of the Welfare State have foisted Entitlement programs upon America, draining the public coffers of funds more productively spent on military buildups and corporate subsidies. Fortunately, leg-islators in the New American Century have scaled back these wretched programs and have replaced them with entitlements for themselves. The government does not fund these programs. Funding is provided by the lobbyists in the form of free dinners, family vacations, green fees and all kinds of perks so necessary for main-taining a smooth running pay as you play government.

Environmentalism: A misguided philosophy inspired by Satan himself. To protect the earth against man's rightful use of all its resources goes against every Biblical precept. God placed everything at man's disposal. To refuse to use it is to refuse a gift from God!

Envy: One of the outmoded Seven Deadly Sins. What one envies is something better than one is or possesses. The world envies America—which is right and proper. How is that bad?

> *"Unjust criticism is usually disguised compliment. It often means that you have aroused jealously and **envy**. Remember that no one ever kicks a dead log."*
>
> —Dale Carnegie

Ethics: The good rules we live by: do unto others before they do it to you, cover your ass and if it makes money, just do it!

For the commoners, the Sermon on the Mount is a great standard by which to live. One must remember that Jesus spoke to the *multitudes*. He did not preach in Herod's palace or at the homes of the wealthy. No, his message was meant for the consumption of the lowly. At other times he even derided the rich: "…for it is easier for a camel to pass through the eye of the needle than for a rich man to get to heaven," yada, yada, yada. That, of course, was a tactic to make inferiors think that they are in some ways actually better than their betters. But he made up for it when he told them to "render unto Caesar that which is Caesar's." The message is clear: keep your nose clean and keep in your place without complaint.

With respect to ethics, the legislative branch of America's government, i.e., the House and the Senate have, as one would imagine, special rules to live by—special rules that hold these lofty individuals at a higher plane of standards than any ordinary mortal man. As such, the three strikes rule is out, thus accounting for Tom Delay's ability to retain his post after three ethics violations. Unfortunately, an indictment by outsiders, i.e., the justice department, is a bit over the top.

Ethnic Cleansing: Genocide of a certain ethnic group unless perpetrated by America or Israel, in which case it is God's will. After all, did not God order the Israelites to rid the area of Caananites? And there are other examples.

Eugenics: The scientific study of the superiority of the Anglo-European and the basis for "culling the herd" in order to protect and strengthen the species. Some people mistake eugenics to be the scientific basis for "white power." This is an error, which for the time being, is best kept as is since a good number of white power advocates are diehard proponents of the New American Century and all of its goals. Eventually, it will become apparent to the hillbilly in-bred riff-raff that just being white certainly does not mean that they are to be included as acceptable breeding stock.

Euro, The: Counterfeit garbage that should be forever destroyed and forgotten before it does serious damage to the dollar.

European Union: A demonic organization bent on rivaling America for economic supremacy. When there were ten members it sure looked like they were the ten horns of the beast in Revelation but we all have to move on. Anyway, they're still a nasty bunch.

Euthanasia: For the present a bad thing. When the New American Century is in full swing there will be a rise in useless eaters and it might be high time to rethink this one. How this will play with our friends on the religious right may be problematic but one must remain optimistic that a new Biblical slant can be generated that will fit the bill.

Everything: The one and only thing America has a right to control.

Evidence: There are two classes of evidence—evidence that is damaging to the New American Century and evidence that damages the enemy. Evidence that damages the New American Century is to be lost, stolen, misplaced, shredded, hidden, challenged, attacked and/or the messenger is to be vilified and hung out to dry. Evidence that damages the enemy may be real or manufactured, to be used without reservation.

Evildoer: A villain, miscreant, knave, blackguard, bad guy, a doer of evil. As well, a terrorist, blue collar criminal, lefty activist, unionist or anyone who opposes the New American Century.

Evolution: Old school nonsense. Creation Science will dispel those silly old myths and restore scholasticism to American schools.

Executive Privilege: A well-deserved right given to our leaders in order to protect them as they do the good work in the secrecy that is necessary. Of course, liberals abuse this privilege to hide their nefarious schemes and so, liberal administrations should rightly be subject to intense scrutiny and undying pressure. (See Sworn Testimony)

Exit Polls: Practices harmful to the new voting system. Getting a statistically accurate count of votes can often lead to conflicts with the preordained outcome. Exit polls must be outlawed.

Exit Strategy: During the Clinton administration it was established that in order for America to wage war one of the necessary prerequisites was to have an exit strategy before going in. The same will hold true under the New American Century but critics of the current war do not seem to understand the new terminology. They protest that America invaded Iraq with "no exit strategy". That is precisely the strategy—no exit. America will not be deserting its new colonies and henceforth there will be a no exit strategy. Verstehen Sie?

Exploitation: Taking advantage of the powerless is the American way.

Extraordinary Rendition: A fine example of outsourcing. Since it is illegal to torture people in America, the next best thing to do is send suspects out of the country for proper handling. This practice is called Extraordinary Rendition, as in extraordinary rendition of US law.

F is for FEDERALISM

Facts: Bothersome details that often must be disputed in order to paint a proper picture. One must always get one's facts straight by claiming as fact anything that promotes the New American Century. Once it has been written down or spoken on TV, then it becomes truth.

FAIR: Imagine a "news" organization that proclaims that there is a Conservative media bias! FAIR, Fairness & Accuracy in Reporting attempts to do just that, unFAIRly spewing its own bias against reporting that is balanced, American and Godlike in its Truth.

Faith: One may put one's faith only in God, family, the free market, the Republican Party and the New American Century. Otherwise, it is misguided and delusional. Faith is one of the Seven Heavenly Virtues and you have to have it or at least pretend you do in order to get anywhere in politics, especially in the Red States.

Faith Based Initiatives: A way for the government not to interfere in religion by funding their private projects, thus freeing funds that can be spent on proselytizing. Religion plays a big part in the New American Century and it is good to reward the faithful. (See Useful Idiots)

Falwell, Jerry (1933–): Famed fundamentalist Baptist televangelist is a triple hitter for the New American Century—God, war and business. Falwell pulls no punches against anything liberal, righteously blaming civil libertarians, feminists, homosexuals, and abortion rights supporters for the terrorist attacks of 9/11. He's a go-to guy for the media. A reliable source if ever there was one.

Family, Spending Time With One's: No appointee who fails miserably in working for the government may quit in disgrace as it reflects poorly upon the Administration for choosing such a loser in the first place. No, the proper way to dispose of oneself (at the urging of one's superiors) is to resign for reasons of

Spending Time With One's Family. This is to be followed by an award ceremony replete with medals, soppy speeches and completely erroneous press releases.

Family Values: A vague, indescribable notion that pretty much sums up a proper moral sense. If you don't know what family values are then you don't have them. If you understand the meaning of family values then you will be blessed by their virtue and you can trust anyone who claims to possess them as well. If a leader speaks of family values then you can and must follow him and be loyal to his every command. If he does not, he must be rejected ASAP.

Fascism: So misunderstood. (See Corporatism)

> *"When fascism comes to America it will be wrapped in the flag and carrying a cross."*

> —Sinclair Lewis

Faulty Intelligence: Faulty Intel is doubly useful: (1) to be used whenever it helps the New American Century and (2) to be used as an example why new and more draconian intelligence gathering measures must be incorporated into the War on Terrorism! Now that we "know" that faulty intelligence led us into Iraq (a good use of (1) above), we must allow illegal wiretaps to be used in order to get better intelligence (a good use of (2) above).

FBI, The: In the New American Century the Federal Bureau of Investigation will have broader powers to investigate opponents of the New American Century. COINTELPRO was just the warm-up for things to come.

FCC, The: The Federal Communications Commission oversees all media in America. In the New American Century, FCC stands for Facilitates Corporate Control.

FDA, The: The Food & Drug Administration is responsible for making sure that drugs and foods are safe for profits. Most of the people who are in charge of the FDA have worked in and will be working in the pharmaceutical or food industry so they know exactly what is expected of them.

Fear: Love's wonderful partner. Fear and Love are the two great motivators. When something is loved there is always the accompanying fear of losing it. Fear stimulates the best in Americanism. Comfort and satisfaction lead only to complacency and letting down one's guard whereas fear primes the cycle of acquisition and security seeking. The most important thing we have to fear is the freedom from fear itself.

God said to fear Him. So it must be good to do if God said we should do it. We should also fear our government, our business leaders, our parents and all manner of authority figures. A healthy dose of fear will keep everybody in line.

"Fear is the foundation of most governments."

—John Adams (1735-1826)

Federalist Society, The: The premier Conservative legal organization in America. While being strict proponents of states rights, they know full well when the federal government should step in and take charge, especially when a state is trammeling the rights of corporations or if a state is allowing people to take too much control over their lives.

FEMA: Federal Emergency Management Agency. FEMA is the agency that controls the situation in any emergency. Should things get out of hand for the upper class, FEMA stands ready to invoke martial law and clamp down on the populace. Under the New American Century, FEMA really stands for **F**ailure to **E**ffectively **M**anage **A**nything. But hey, what can you expect from an agency run by an ousted horse show manager named Brownie who got tagged because he was the college roommate of the previous guy?

Feminism: The self-congratulatory refuge of lesbians, witches, man-haters, abortionists, midwives and defilers of the natural order of things. Also know as Feminazis, Feminists despise their own sex and suffer from "penis envy". To be feminine is a different matter. In the New American Century, the ideal woman would be someone like Ann Coulter or Beverly LeHay.

Few Bad Apples: Whenever things go awry it is necessary to scapegoat some of the lower echelons and blame the whole debacle on them. (See also Plausible Denial)

Filibuster, The: An old Senatorial gimmick used to combat the "tyranny of the majority." Since Republicans now constitute the majority the filibuster is an outrageous trick by notorious and scandalous Democrats attempting to promote a tyranny of the minority.

FISA: Foreign Intelligence Surveillance Act of 1978—a precursor to the New American Century that paves the way to trashing the 4th Amendment, allowing expanded snooping and wiretapping capabilities of the government. A FISA court issues warrants at the drop of a hat to any agency interested in getting the goods on someone—retroactively, if necessary. That is, the snooping proceeds and the permission is granted afterwards. Even though the court denied permission only a few times out of thousands of requests, it is considered a nuisance in the New American Century and has been circumvented by Presidential decree. Now, **FISA** stands for **F**inally **I**nvestigating **S**ecretly **A**nytime.

Fishing: There's an old saying that you can give a man a fish and feed him that day but if you teach him how to fish he can feed himself every day. That was all well and good but from now on, you can forget about the free fish and you'd better be one of the "players" because as fishing holes become more and more scarce only the inside few will be allowed to sport.

Flag, The: Old Glory—the symbol of America. It's to the Flag one pledge's allegiance and not the constitution.

Flag Burning: One of the perennial diversions in the grab bag of political obfuscation. Flag burning in America is so rare as to almost be non-existent. Nevertheless, it must be reported as epidemic as we near any election because nothing riles a good American like the thought of Old Glory being desecrated.

Flag Waving: The patriotic thing to do whenever war breaks out. Oddly, waving a Confederate flag shows how ultra-patriotic you are.

Flat Tax: Nothing could be fairer to low income Americans than to be able to pay their fair share of taxes the same as the wealthy do. In addition, there would be a sizeable simple deduction that would all but eliminate any tax burden on the really strapped. Of course, once a flat tax system is in place, that deduction can easily be tweaked whenever necessary.

Flip-Flop: Liberals are all over the map with their situational ethics and fit-to-please politics. Now, not *everything* is written in stone and when a Conservative changes his or her mind it is through thoughtful reconsideration and demonstrates maturity.

FOIA, The: The Freedom of Information Act—a seditious law that undermines the government's ability to keep secrets. Fortunately, National Security trumps FOIA and a conscientious public servant will redact any information some snooping liberal is after way before he gets there. FOIA has been emasculated to the point where it stands for **FOI**led **A**gain.

Follow the Money: Forget this foolishness. Follow the rhetoric. It is so much more peaceful and pleasant if people would just do as they say, not as they do.

In Iraq, following the money is impossible. Everything there is currently done on a cash and carry basis (all the cash you can carry) with no receipts.

Fool Me Once…: Famous saying originating from Texas but well known as far as Tennessee: "Fool me once, shame on shame on you. Fool me—you can't get fooled again." In context, President Bush used this old saw to let the American people know that Saddam had tricked us into thinking he didn't have WMD's when he really didn't and because we thought he really did but didn't then we weren't going to let him trick us again.

Force: Something Americans fully understand. Therefore, the only thing our enemies are going to get.

Foreign Aid: So misunderstood by the average American. Foreign Aid is not designed as a charity handout to rag-tag nations, although a small percentage is earmarked to that end for public relations purposes. The vast majority of Foreign Aid funds are sent with enormous strings attached. Primarily, the recipients are to use the monies to buy certain American goods so that in effect, Foreign Aid is using public funds to increase the profits of targeted American corporations. Secondly, any country receiving Foreign Aid has to know on which side the bread is buttered when it comes to crucial UN votes. Witness how much the duplicitous Yemeni vote against the invasion of Iraq has cost that country!

Foreign Policy: America's foreign policy is to use our military and economic might to persuade other nations to our way of thinking. When other countries use coercion and bullying it is a threat to the stability of the world unless, of course, they are our allies and are doing something that we approve of.

Forgiveness: To err is human, to forgive divine. Since no one in the New American Century is divine there is no need for forgiveness nor shall there be any. For those who do harm in the name of progress there is the pardon. For those who slight the dawning empire there is nothing but retribution.

Fortitude: The Heavenly Virtue of having guts. Americans have plenty of guts.

Fossil Record, The: A whole lot of bones have been dug up that mislead people into thinking that the earth is old and that evolution is real. Obviously, Satan has planted these bones in order to dupe those willing to be duped.

Fox Guarding the Henhouse, The: A euphemism for a political appointee to a position where instead of safeguarding the populace against all sorts of corporate chicanery, said appointee operates in the sole interest of business. In the New American Century all henhouses will be *required* to have foxes guarding them.

Fox News Network, The: Leading proponents and a shining example of everything that stands for the New American Century. The No Spin Zone of Fox will not allow any heretical views to spin their way onto the airwaves. In its fair and balanced reporting it will bring on dissenters but the viewer can rest assured that this is only to rebut and ridicule their positions. One can rely on Fox to report the way things are meant to be.

France: A land in Old Europe of snail eating, spineless, unwashed, ungrateful foreigners that we have to keep rescuing. For two hundred plus years France was our staunch ally but when they didn't throw in with us against Saddam they threw our friendship away. The fact that French soldiers are still involved in Afghanistan has no bearing on our enmity towards them.

Franken, Al: Another one of those liberal talk-show hosts on Air America. Franken is a real wise guy who says he supports the troops but not the mission—whatever that means. Unlike Bill O'Reilly, Franken is willing to desert his post as announcer to go off on USO shows and entertain the troops. Who says running off to who-cares-where (Afghanistan and Iraq) and talking to a handful of GI's is better than staying home and keeping up the good banter with millions of listeners in the safety of one's studio?

Can you believe the chutzpah of this guy talking about running for a senatorial slot in Minnesota? Well, if he wins it will at least get him off the air and less people will be exposed to his wit and humor.

Freedom: Freedom is a concept that is apprehended differently by people depending upon many factors. Freedom in the New American Century will be unambiguous. One will be free to do almost anything except transgress against the New American Century whose laws and tenets need not be enumerated here for they are legion.

Freedom Fries: German Fries before the Hun went crazy in WWI (when we first had to rescue the Frogs). Now you can only get Freedom Fries in the congressional cafeteria because French Fries are nasty and it is politically incorrect to order or eat them.

Freedom Fighter: Anyone fighting for a cause that America approves. (Contrast with Terrorist)

Free Press: That which is necessary for a vibrant and informed populace. In other words, something to be despised and thanks to twenty-five years of reforming communications law the Free Press has been relegated to the "Underground". (See also Self-Censorship)

Free Speech Zone: An out of the way place where demonstrators and other troublemakers can go and rant to their hearts' content. No one is going to hear or see except Homeland Security.

Freepers: FreeRepublic.com's web warriors. Electronic storm troopers for the New American Century. Freepers make the crank calls to lefty talking heads, do the right wing blogs and keep the media polls tilted in the right direction.

Free Trade: The right of corporations to do business across international borders without any impediments. Wherever impediments to free trade are encountered, America is obligated to subsidize the multi-nationals so as to keep their profits at a satisfactory level.

Frist, Bill: Our current Senate Majority Leader and a real medical doctor no less! In fact, Mr. Frist is able to make snap diagnoses just by looking at a video of the patient, as he did by declaring Terry Schiavo fully awake and responding after viewing a few seconds of tape. One might even say he is a faith diagnostician.

Frivolous Lawsuits: While it is necessary and right that corporations should protect themselves as, for example, does Wal-Mart in suing K-Mart over the use of rotating checkout carousels or Kellogg's lawsuit against a golf course over using the word "toucan", it is shameful and a waste of taxpayer dollars when a person or group sues a corporation for knowingly selling and distributing harmful products or for willfully destroying the ecosystem. Class action suits are especially egregious. Therefore, it is imperative that reform be instituted to protect industry from the populace. Take heart, torte reform is on the way!

Fundraising: In order to run for office, one must either be rich or have rich friends who are willing to put up a stake. Once in office, fundraising in order to build up a "war chest" for the next election pretty much takes up all of one's time. Not a problem. All one has to do is delegate authority and be there to vote when and how it counts, i.e., in one's donors' best interests. Forgetting this could be a fatal error.

G is for GOD

Gannon, Jeff: A.k.a. James Dale Guckert, this fine young man was a shining beacon of truth in the Washington Press Corps, asking both the President and Scott McClellan the hard questions about liberals and bringing to the fore the great work the administration was doing in virtually every facet of life. When the going got tough at news briefings, Jeff was the go-to guy to help set the tone and change the pace.

Who outed this wonderful man of principle as a male prostitute? It looks like clones of Deep Throat are doing rear guard actions against fine journalists in attempts to smear the White House.

GAO, The: The Government Accountability Office, a completely annoying branch of Congress that keeps putting out numbers on all facets of governmental programs that don't match the one's put out by the White House.

Gated Community: If the riff-raff can have affordable housing it isn't going to be inside of a gated community. This is preferential housing and one must be able to pay the freight in order to reap the benefits of security and seclusion.

Gays: We love you all but hate the sin. No one is born gay—being gay is totally a choice. Now, if you would just stop trying to get married and get yourselves back into the closet we could get to those good old days we're aiming for. Don't you realize that if we were to actually acknowledge you people that it would mean the breakdown of everything? Our whole society would fall apart! We are on the verge of the Apocalypse and you are messing things up.

Generation X: Those who were born in America from 1965 to 1980. Most of Gen X will miss the boat on the military aspects of the New American Century. However, those who are involved are in the upper echelons of command and are poised to take the helm as soon as the Boomers get out of the way.

Genocide: When bad people kill a lot of people it is genocide. When good people kill a lot of people it is either good riddance or collateral damage. (See Ethnic Cleansing)

Get Out of Jail Free Card, The: One is issued to the well born at birth.

Global Warming: An insidious myth promoted by America haters and Luddites. There are a few weather anomalies and worrying hot spots that one must concede will require a few decades of research in order to establish that they are of natural origin.

God: The Creator of everything who selected the Hebrews as his Chosen People and who clearly favors America right now. Apart from being omnipotent, omniscient, omnipresent and all the other omni's, God is pretty much like a tough-loving grandpa who kicks ass and takes names. If you're coming from the Heartland you've got a leg up on being in God's good graces because you were brought up right.

Of course, many confused people make up their own version of God. Liberals can't stomach the idea of Hell so they believe in some squishy, touchy-feely everybody's going to some great reward nonsense. That's why they think they can do just anything they want and get away with it. They're in for a big surprise come the Judgment Day. Then there's all the heathen religions that are even worse. They'll all burn, too.

Goering, Herman (1893–1946): Hitler's second in command—another inspiration to the New American Century. At the Nuremburg trials, Goering candidly stated, "Of course the people don't want war. But after all, it's the leaders of the country who determine the policy, and it's always a simple matter to drag the people along whether it's a democracy, a fascist dictatorship, or a parliament, or a communist dictatorship. Voice or no voice, the people can always be brought to the bidding of the leaders. That is easy. All you have to do is tell them they are being attacked, and denounce the pacifists for lack of patriotism, and exposing the country to greater danger."

Golden Parachute: When an executive descends from the Olympian heights of international finance and corporate boardrooms to alight gracefully on the plains of Eternal Wealth, the Golden Parachute facilitates a happy landing.

Sometimes, however, executives leap from spire to spire, eschewing the delights of retirement. In such cases it is more appropriate to speak of a Golden Hang Glider whereby one may soar secure in the knowledge that the corporate safety net lies permanently below.

Gonzales, Alberto R., Judge: GW Bush's second Attorney General. This plucky little Hispanic judge has been helping GW for years, including, as council to then Governor Bush, helping GW get out of jury duty so he could escape having to answer embarrassing questions about previous DUI's. Gonzales' pro-torture stance made him a shoe-in for the berth vacated by John Ashcroft.

Goodman, Amy: Host of Democracy Now, a radio and TV news program broadcast over 350 stations and author of "Exception to the Rulers." Ms. Goodman refuses to shill for the New American Century—the quickest way for any newscaster to make the big bucks. Her continued exposure of sleights perpetrated by the Bush Administration make her one of the most dangerous commie pinkos in the news business. Real Americans would do well to ignore this woman and tune in to Fox where one may be untroubled by the facts.

Good Old Days, The: Liberals and scoffers like to say that there weren't any Good Old Days in America but there was a time—and it wasn't so long ago—that being free, white and 21 meant something! Those were the Good Old Days and by God we are going to make things right in the future!

Gott Mit Uns: Soldiers of the Wehrmacht wore belt buckles emblazoned with the slogan, Gott Mit Uns—God is with us. Well, they were wrong. God is with America. Gott mit die Vereinigten Staaten!

Government: Actually a good thing when kept to a proper size. While it has no capacity for doing anything right it is nevertheless necessary to safeguard the rights of business by keeping a weather eye on those who would infringe upon those rights. It is also useful in coordinating and bearing the costs for research and development, ensuring a reasonably well educated work force, propping up Wall Street whenever necessary, socializing and monitoring the populace and providing cannon fodder to protect business interests worldwide. Big government is fine as long as it confines itself to these ends.

Greatest Generation, The: Americans who lived during and participated in the Great Depressions and World War II. Now they are all retired and are sucking the country dry on their Social Security.

Greed: A healthy feeling toward possessions—the will to acquire more and more. Greed has historically been touted as one of the "Seven Deadly Sins" (under the name Avarice) but that is for the consumption of the masses to keep them from aspiring to get a piece of the action. Let the little man keep to his delusions. Greed is a great motivator. It drives our system.

> *"What kind of society isn't structured on greed? The problem of social organization is how to set up an arrangement under which greed will do the least harm; capitalism is that kind of system."*
>
> —Milton Friedman

Green Party, The: A bunch of tree-hugging fruit wads that provide an incalculable service to America by siphoning off votes from the Democrats. Greens stand in direct opposition to God's natural law and the dominion of man over everything. Greens are really Reds.

Gridlock: When Democrats disagree with Republicans and use stalling tactics, vetoes, hide legislation in committee, etc. there is gridlock and the good business of government cannot be accomplished. When Republicans stall Democrats it is for the good of the nation and the will of God.

Guatanamo: The base at Guantanamo Bay, a.k.a. "Gitmo" is where terrorists are confined in legal limbo. Gitmo is really the property of Cuba but completely controlled by America so if anything bad happens there it's Castro's fault.
  The terrorists, some as young as 13 were originally housed at Camp X-Ray, a bunch of chain link boxes originally built for Haitian boat people. It turned out that Camp X-Ray was a bit too brutal for the terrorists so they have been removed to a more hospitable Camp Delta. Apparently, Camp X-Ray was good enough for the Haitians.

Gullibility: A wonderful attribute of the American people—to be fully exploited.

Gun Control: The rights of the citizens to bear arms will not be abridged. Nuf said.

Guns: To quote Charleton Heston, guns are "instruments of love." And, boy howdy, we do love our guns! Tough love because guns are tough and so are Americans. You got a gun and you're somebody—not some sissified, emasculated Euro-boy.

H is for HOMELAND SECURITY

Habeas Corpus: The outmoded, costly and inefficient right to a trial. Anybody that gets himself arrested must be guilty of something.

Habitat for Humanity: A group of do-gooder attention seekers who ruin neighborhoods by housing people who haven't paid their full dues.

Haiti: One of the most dangerous rogue nations on the planet. Haitians continually get uppity and try to gain their insidious independence *right in America's own hemisphere*! They just don't seem to be able to elect proper leaders and must therefore be constantly chaperoned. America's policies toward Haiti are completely shared with the French because it was French incompetence that let the Haitians get out of control in the first place.

Halliburton: One of the premier companies in America. Halliburton (which once, by the way, had Dick Cheney as its CEO) can do just about everything. That's why it has received so many no-bid contracts in Iraq and New Orleans. A lot of crying crybabies holler and scream about this fine company getting these perks but no other company is in such a distinctive position—uniquely qualified to underserve our troops and overcharge for doing it.

Hannity, Sean: Robust and comely god of smarm and loquacity in the pantheon of the New American Century. Cherubic in form, Hannity nevertheless comes on like an avenging seraph. Liberals and other America haters who try to go up against this Foxy talk show host will find themselves "Hannitized"—taken to the cleaners and talked over with vigor and single-minded determination. Nothing but the sweet right escapes from those fulsome lips. Justifiably, he was named TV's sexiest newscaster by Playgirl Magazine.

Happiness, The Pursuit of: The Declaration of Independence clearly states that man is endowed with inalienable rights. To whit: life, liberty and the pursuit of happiness. Now, the founding fathers originally wanted to say life, liberty and the pursuit of *property* but that was dropped. However, since the pursuit and, of course, acquisition of property brings happiness, the use of the term "happiness" can be seen as an "umbrella" for going out and getting all you can in order to obtain happiness. One could then paraphrase: life, liberty and the pursuit of property, profit, empire, power, dominion, wealth, social heights, etc.

Hate Crime: A classification of crimes invented by liberals, gays, heathens and minorities in order to claim that they are special victims just because somebody doesn't like them and that makes the crime more heinous than "regular" crime. They want you to think that a person who keys a gay man's car because he won't stop coming on to him is worse than a rapist!

Hawk: Slang for a pro-war patriot. An apt metaphor since the hawk is a fierce and noble creature. (Contrast with Dove)

Healthy Forest Initiative, The: A healthy forest is one that doesn't stand in the way of progress, New American Century style. Wood can burn so it is imperative to remove as much as humanly possible. Since large lumber companies are best equipped to do the job, the government is doing all it can to hire them to doctor up the backwoods. Furthermore, there are other natural resources that need to be exploited out there in the boonies and trees are in the way of getting there. Besides, as President Reagan told us, "Trees cause more pollution than automobiles do." And his Secretary of the Interior James Watt is rumored to have said, "We don't have to protect the environment, the Second Coming is at hand." That's a one-two punch at the forests that'll be sure to knock them out!

Heartland, The: A synonym for Middle America, the wheat belt, down home, country. Anyplace in America except the coastal and northern big cities. The red states. (See Homeland)

Heathen: An unbeliever—one who rejects the principles of the New American Century. One who does not ascribe to supply side economics, the rights of privilege, Pax Americana and empire, the Culture of Life, and the sanctity of all that is American.

Heaven: The place that God has reserved for (true) Christian Conservatives in the afterlife. Good Americans—mostly from the Heartland, will heavily populate Heaven. God's gated community.

Hegemony: A fancy word for supremacy. America rules or America is Number One are easier ways of saying the same thing. Few people pronounce Hegemony correctly so it is better to leave such words to the experts.

Hell: Where everybody but (true) Christian Conservatives are going in the afterlife. There are some really good hearted, likeable folks who don't believe in Jesus the right way but think that they'll make it to heaven. This is just a sad myth.

Heretic: Anyone who perverts the essence of any New American Century ideal—a closet deformer. A person may follow each and every creed of the NAC except, for example, backslide on the notion that one must reduce taxes during wartime. That is enough to make them a Heretic.

Hidey-Hole: A tiny bunker—a place where rats go to hide from the light of day. Saddam was ~~placed~~ found in a hidey-hole.

History: History will look kindly toward the New American Century as the most positive force mankind has ever experienced. Naturally, unbiased proponents will write this history. And it certainly does not hurt the cause to replace the National Archivist with one of the boys, namely Mr. Allen Weinstein, who managed to buy his way into exclusive rights to KGB documentation, keeping it to himself—something of an ethics violation. Yep, history will look kindly toward this lofty period once written by the right folks.

Hitchens, Christopher: In the pantheon of the New American Century, Christopher Hitchens is the penultimate Bacchanalian figure. Having once been a diehard hardhead for the left he has reemerged—been reborn, as it were—as an unapologetic apologist for everything good and noble. Hitchens uses his considerable powers of logic to accuse all those opposed to the invasion of Iraq as secret admirers and wholehearted supporters of Saddam Hussein. Indeed, anyone who disagrees with Mr. Hitchens must be exposed as having given themselves over to the dark side.

Hitler, Adolf (1889–1945): Der Fuhrer, the Chancellor of Germany and dictator from 1933 until his death. Adolf Hitler is the poster boy for evil and comparing anyone to him is to declare them a ruthless murdering despot and a monster of the worst kind. That having been said, a lot of the ideas and methods of Hitler and his cohorts are quite appealing, especially in the areas of propaganda, population control and government. While the New American Century distances itself without qualification from Hitler, one must always be open minded enough to admit that even the worst of us has some good points. Admittedly, he made mistakes. Here is an example of his wrong thinking: "There could be no issue between the Church and the State. The Church, as such, has nothing to do with political affairs. On the other hand, the State has nothing to do with the faith or inner organization of the Church."

Hollygon: Today's modern military is equipped with its own film studios and teams of public relations journalists. If it can be staged in order to pump up the troops or inspire the folks back home, Hollygon can get the job done. (See Jessica Lynch)

Home Grown Terrorist: Unlikely as it seems, the prime suspect in acts of terrorism on America's soil is a white guy, usually a vet—but that isn't going to deter us from rousting towel-heads, minorities or any other suspicious un-American types.

Homeland Security: A boon to the security industry. Obviously, a pretty much useless endeavor since it is well nigh impossible to keep a weather eye on all our porous borders. Still, it is necessary to keep up appearances. And everyone knows that a good defense is a good offense so what we generally do is stick it to them in their own back yard. The true meaning and goal of homeland security is to safeguard the property and persons of the ruling elite.

Homeland, The: Mostly the Heartland but grudgingly included are the blue states since we need them to take the brunt of any terrorist attacks and also to provide America with entertainment and to keep the economy afloat.

Homeless, The: Hobos, bums, vagrants, gypsies, tramps, vagabonds, drifters, indigents, nomads, untrainables, migrants, i.e., those who have opted out of the Ownership Society and prefer camping and begging to doing an honest day's work.

Homosexuality: One expects liberals to be gay due to their permissive, perverted lifestyles and beliefs. However, it is a well-known fact that there are a number of conservative homo-sexuals and the truth be told, the New American Century is ambivalent toward private sexual preferences. That having been said, in deference to the religious right, gay bashing is in. Besides, conservative gays are manly, not girly-fem, limp-wristed sister boys like their liberal counterparts. Angry and gay, that's OK!

Honesty: Honesty used to sell but no one is buying it anymore. Everyone suspects everyone else of having something up his sleeve so that today, honesty is openly admitting to dishonesty in order to earn respect and trust. Of course, for the really egregious trespasses the best policy is, as always, not getting caught.

Honor: In this day and age, honor can get you into a peck of trouble. Standing up for what's right, having the gumption to go against the flow is nothing more than the kind of self-congratulatory flooflorall that will earn you at best the admiration of those who don't matter and at worst, retribution from the folks that do.

House/Senate Ethics: Elected officials, being self-regulated must be held to a different set of rules as the common herd. Whereas a citizen is chastised when he breaks the law—or runs afoul of the law in some way—a Representative or Senator is subject to a pack of rules unique to their respective assemblages. For the most part, these rules concern themselves with how a member comports himself. Out and out bribery is not condoned. Dueling has been abolished and flagrant abuses of power will not be tolerated. However, subtle forms of the aforesaid are fair game and as each party gains the upper hand it is able to modify certain rules in order to best get away with unseemly practices. In the New American Century, rules favoring the Republican agenda are to be carried out to the letter and ethics is to be supplanted by Darwinian rules of the jungle.

Hubris: Hubris is an essential quality of the President and his Cabinet Members for it imbues them with righteousness coupled and a total lack of fear of the people. Representatives would do well to acquire this quality so as to do the good work of the New American Century with disregard for their constituent's needs and wishes.

Humanism: Centering on people, worrying about their needs, caring for their general welfare and making attempts to live in harmony is Satanic. God will look after all of us.

Humanitarian Aid: Money forced to be spent for public relations purposes following a natural disaster or a long, long drought.

Humiliation: Although it does not aid in the interrogation process, humiliation is one of the standard procedures. It usually leads to intransigence and deep resentment but it does entertain the guards.

Humility: The art of affecting a humble demeanor in the public forum. Humility clashes with an ostentatious lifestyle and so, arrogance is the much preferred method of interfacing with the mob.

Hundredth Monkey Theory, The: From watching monkeys wash their food. Apparently, monkeys on a Japanese island used to eat wild yams *au natural* until one day a female named Ito washed hers in the surf, thus cleaning off the sand and adding a little salt to boot. Anyway, after more and more monkeys became familiar with this technique on the island a strange thing happened: monkeys of this type all over the world began washing their food. So, the 100th Monkey Theory is the idea that once a sufficient number of members of a group start doing something new, the whole group picks up the change.

Now all of this sounds pretty New Agey, spacey-wacey and indeed, the fluff-headed left thinks that they can change everybody over to their way of thinking just by having enough people do their mantras or whatever. Don't worry. Even if it does work there are already far more people kicking back with a brew in front of the TV every night and that's a habit that's pretty much here to stay.

Hurricane Katrina: This storm was an obvious Act of God intended to punish the denizens of a wicked city. Unfortunately for those who live in outlying areas and neighboring states, God indulges Himself in wreaking a bit of collateral damage. FEMA's slow reaction to the devastation has been totally misrepresented by the liberal media in an attempt to besmirch the wonderful job Brownie did. As an Act of God it was the right and humble duty of FEMA of step aside and not interfere with the plans of the Almighty.

Hybrid Cars: Hybrid Cars utilize both the standard internal combustion engine and the electric motor in such a way as to self-charge and greatly decrease gas consumption. They are anathema to the oil industry and legislation must therefore be put into place that makes it impractical to own one. Currently, in order to make up for loss of revenues associated with gasoline taxes, our fine lawmakers are toying with the idea of a mileage tax, effectively neutralizing one advantage for the hybrid owner. Also, there are all sorts of discounts and even tax rebates available for picking up an SUV.

Hydra: The Hydra was a mythological beast that had the ability to grow two heads where one had been severed. Al Qaeda is like the many-headed Hydra because everything we do to diminish their number just seems to increase the threat.

Hydraulic Fracturing: This is a tried and true method of squeezing oil and gas out of old mother earth. You just pump a mess of liquids into the ground under tremendous pressure and crack things wide-open way underneath. Unfortunately, the stuff you pump in stays there and messes up the ground water but when it comes to getting oil you've got to get your priorities straight.

Hypocrite: One who castigates another for actions that one also engages in. Like they say, "Don't knock it until you've tried it." Or, "It takes one to know one." Therefore, hypocrisy is in fact a form of honesty, totally useful in politics. Today's Hypocrite may stand up shamelessly and denounce others (for the things they are themselves guilty) as long as the party being denounced is an enemy of the New American Century.

Jesus derided the Hypocrites but that was a long time ago and about a bunch of high-handed Jews. He urged them to pray in private and not pretend to religious zeal just for a public show. Well, maybe that didn't play so hot in old Jerusalem but it goes great over the airwaves on C-Span, CBN or TBN.

I is for IDEOLOGY

Ideology: There are all kinds of ideologies—all but a few are false. The ideology behind the New American Century is the correct ideology to have. All other ideologies are counterproductive, insane, false and will ultimately get you into trouble. Avoid them at all costs!

IED's: Improvised Explosive Devices—these nasty booby traps are responsible for most of the American deaths in Iraq. Apparently, Iraqi insurgents are able to build ever more sophisticated homemade bombs out of scarce resources—or maybe these things are part of Saddam's arsenal that we failed to guard and went missing soon after our victory was accomplished.

Ignorance: Ignorance is bliss and education in the New American Century is interested in the happiness of the American people.

Imagination: A dangerous form of thought indicating that one has too much time on one's hands. The people must avoid using imagination at all costs as it leads to speculating about things they haven't been told. Preventative measures include watching television, listening to talk radio or reading magazines about movie stars.

IMF, The: The International Monetary Fund—the bank of free trade and loan sharks to the third world. Along with the World Bank and other large lenders, the IMF has steadily pumped money into poor countries in the hopes that they will either pay back the loans or default and be forced to give up their natural resources in lieu of payments.

Immigration: The proper and legal way in which America gets the best and brightest from the outside. Legal immigrants are really Americans that were just unlucky they were born elsewhere.

Immoral: Anything contrary to family values. Public officials caught engaging in immoral behavior are to be summarily dismissed or censured. Past immoral behavior brought to light can be redressed in two ways: (1) chalked up to youthful indiscretion, (2) as having been before one was "born again". Using either of these two strategies—or better yet both—will invariably put past transgressions to rest. Naturally, liberals who profess to having turned a new leaf cannot be trusted in the least. Once red, always red.

Impeachment: What must be done to those in public office who commit high crimes and misdemeanors with the exception, of course, of those who stray beyond the normal bounds in order to promote Americanism.

Impulse Buying: A freedom thanks to the faith of credit companies in the American consumer.

Income Tax: The good tax levied on wages. Bad taxes are levied against capital gains, inheritance and interest income.

Indian Giver: A derogatory term used to describe someone who goes back on his or her word. Obviously derived from having given land to the Indians under treaty and then taking the land away from the Indians by breaking the treaties, but the term "White Man Giver" is too offensive, thus the preferred alternative.

Indifference: The lack of concern for the plight of others that is essential to the New American Century, for it immunizes the populace against caring whether their own rights are being trammeled.

Indigenous Peoples: Indolent squatters on land rich in natural resources that don't have the savvy to exploit it.

Individualism: The rugged archetypical ideal of Americanism. In reality, everyone depends upon one another for support but it is a useful myth to promote the idea of going it alone, pulling one up by one's own bootstraps and such silliness. That way, people are less likely to be sympathetic to those who could use a helping hand, for once you have a society that is willing to work together you are on the slippery slope to socialism at best, out and out communism at worst.

Indulgences: Originally, the idea of an Indulgence stemmed from the notion that a person could shorten his or her time in Purgatory if he or she performed an especially meritorious act for the Church. As with all good intentions, the idea degenerated into something of a shakedown on wealthy parishioners by (the Church) claiming that monetary donations would cut down time in Purgatory for an ancestor or anyone named. Indulgences were far from being biblical and were something of the straw that broke the camel's back, Church historically speaking. They were a great part in sparking the Protestant Reformation of the early 16th century.

Nowadays, political parties have their own form of Indulgence, that being the campaign contribution. Originally—and for the most part, typically—a wealthy corporation would give monetary donations to political campaigns so that the victor of the race would indulge the donor with special laws, contracts and the like. However, this practice has degenerated to the point where politicians are shaking down all but the most powerful by "demanding" contributions lest they be forced to enact legislation harmful to recalcitrant holdouts. In the gangland vernacular of the 1920's, this was also known as "protection" money. In 1517, Martin Luther sparked the Reformation by posting his 95 Theses on the door of the castle church in Wittenburg. One wonders how and when the revolt will come about against the robber barons in Washington, DC.

Industry Watchdogs: A charming metaphor for the viciousness of governmental regulatory services. In the New American Century, the kennels of industrial regulation are going to be wiped clean, replaced by Industry Doormen, ushers who will guide in a new relationship between business and the environment.

Infantile: Jesus wanted for us "to suffer the little children unto him, for theirs is the kingdom of Heaven." What he meant was for us to have childlike minds and that certainly is within keeping of the New American Century, especially in our emotional lives. Children are easily led and tend to believe what they're told. Therefore, it is incumbent upon any good governmental agency to promote infantilism.

Infidelity: Infidelity—cheating on one's spouse—shows a great lack of moral character and fault in one's judgment. Once this heinous act has been committed it must stain the individual for life as it is so often a repeated offense. Politicians who engage in such dalliance are not to be trusted unless, of course, they are

Conservative in which case, infidelity is either an instance of youthful indiscretion (understandable) or the person is just a forgivable rascal.

Infrastructure, The: If it ain't broke, don't fix it. If it's a little broke, either ignore it or put on a band-aid. If it's really broke, make it a state issue. Right now, the Infrastructure is just going to have to be on the back burner because we've got a war on terrorism and a huge military buildup to worry about.

Initiations: The ritual of putting new members of an organization through embarrassing ordeals, a little S&M and incriminating acts in order to secure their silence and loyalty through MAD—mutually assured destruction.

Initiative Process, The: A way for state legislatures to obfuscate and fob the responsibility of passing tough laws onto the voters.

Innocence: In America, one is presumed innocent until arrested and/or put on television. The American sense of justice is thus: We would rather hang one hundred innocent men rather than let one guilty man go free.

Inquisition: Any investigation into any facet of the New American Century.

Insecurity: For the leaders, it is necessary to cultivate a level of Insecurity lest they become lax or worse, lenient. Everything that poses the slightest threat to the stability of the status quo must been seen as a peril of the utmost significance and is to be nipped in the bud with extreme prejudice. Oh, how many of the mighty have fallen because they let down their guard? A good dose of Insecurity keeps one on one's toes.

For the masses, a small measure of Insecurity will go a long way to keep them confused and willing to work against their own interests.

Insider Trading: A right of the wealthy that has been demonized and criminalized by the unworthy. If one cannot confide in one's friends, what kind of society are we creating? Every man gives his friends and neighbors "tips" on sales, bargains and the like. Such confidences are common and natural. What is wrong with their being on a scale fit to one's station in life?

Insubstantial: The claims of environmentalists, liberals and enemies of America.

Insurance: Institutionalized gambling wherein one hedges one's bet against calamity to life, limb, property or just about anything. If one can bet on it, there is a bookmaker in London or Hartford ready to give odds.

Integrity: Integrity is fine and noble but if you have the kind of integrity, say like Atticus Finch in *To Kill A Mockingbird*, you are a bit too straight laced for the New American Century. Integrity is best exemplified in Colin Powell—a good front but willing to do anything you're told. Actually, it's the integrity of the persona put forward that matters, not the person beneath.

Intellectual Property: The real right to life movement—the patenting of living organisms.

Intelligent Design: There are two camps in the Intelligent Design camp. One is a nutball theory created by appeasers who want to bridge the gap between Biblical Truth and Darwinian nonsense in a mish-mash of science and old earth theory. They've got the God part right but that's all.

The true believers (and those in the know) know that there's just too much complexity in the universe for it all to be random. Ergo, it was all created by Jehovah, God of the Hebrew Bible and the Bible (especially the New Testament) is inerrant and is the whole Truth and nothing but the Truth. Why? Because it says so in the Bible!

Interest: One kind of interest is the interest you get on investments. Another kind of interest is when you have a stake in something. That stake is usually in some way connected with gain or at least averting a loss.

> *"I know [patriotism] exists, and I know it has done much in the present contest. But a great and lasting war can never be supported on this principle alone. It must be aided by a prospect of interest, or some reward."*
>
> —George Washington (1732–1799)

Internets, **The**: When GW said "Internets" he wasn't mistaken. There *are* several *Internets*. There's the one that businesses use to sell their goods and services. There's the one that people use to communicate with each other and there's the one that liberals use to spread their filthy lies.

Interview: There are two types of media interview—friendly and confrontational—both of which are conducted most skillfully when the interviewer is in total control. Friendly interviews highlight personality and stay away from controversy of any kind. If that is not possible, the interviewer must spin any controversy in a positive light while the interviewee simply agrees. Confrontational interviews are reserved for liberals and the like. Such interviews are to be conducted so that the interviewee has no time to fully answer any questions. If possible, the interview is then to be edited and statements chopped up and taken out of context in order to reflect badly upon the interviewee.

Iran: Originally Persia, now the second Axis of Evil controlled by zealous religious fundamentalists who ascribe to the wrong religion. Iran has been a real thorn in our side ever since we helped overthrow the elected government and installed our buddy, the Shah, who made the mistake of not leaving a strong enough heir to take over when he died. Now the place is a mess and it looks like we have to fix it again.

Iraq: The first of the Axis of Evil to fall to the conquering heroes of America. Soon Iraq will be the model for the Middle East—a freedom loving democracy forever grateful to America for having saved them from the clutches of that Hitler, Saddam Hussein. Oh, the songs of triumph and glory that shall be born in the breasts of a freed and thankful people. Oh, the everlasting bonds of brotherhood formed between two nations; one the kindly superpower who sacrificed her sons and daughters in selfless disregard of world opinion to liberate the other, a once proud but broken nation. Yes, freedom now rings for the first time in the cradle of civilization thanks to the divine will.

Irony: Irony stems from an incongruity between what might be expected and what actually occurs, as in President Bush's use of irony when he exhorted Syria to withdraw from Lebanon because it would be impossible for them to hold free elections while under occupation. This, of course, on the heels of a highly touted election in occupied Iraq.

IRS, The: In the New American Century, the Internal Revenue Service will remain the premier boogeyman of the citizenry. Anyone who attempts to thwart, reveal, counteract or cast any aspersions upon the new normalcy will find themselves the target of an IRS audit. That will be just the shot across the bow. Repeat offenders will be charged with terrorism.

If in the future a simple flat tax can be enacted, the IRS will simply morph into the nation's collection agency, the **Inland Repo Service.**

Islam: A religion loosely related to Judeo-Christianity but totally different. Islam is all about violence so it is up to Christians to give them some.

Isolationism: A defunct, ostrich-headed philosophy continually sported by our far right brethren. We have to engage the world and bend it to our will. Resting on our laurels in fortress America is well and good but then how will we exploit our southern neighbors if we don't project power globally? C'mon, Pat Buchanan, get with the program!

Israel: The centerpiece of American foreign policy. Propping up Israel is America's duty as it is the only nation capable of maintaining peace and stability in the Middle East through war, violence, retribution and volatility.

J is for JINGOISM

Jesus: Jesus is Lord and if you don't believe it you are going to Hell! Jesus said a lot of things but died too young. Luckily, Saul of Tarsus lived long enough to clarify the fine points and put them in their proper perspective. Also, you can thank Augustine, Thomas Aquinas, Luther, Calvin and many others for putting the proper spin on the why's and where-fore's of all things, turning Christians into the harmonious group you see today.

Jesusland: The blasphemous left is trying to ridicule the Heartland by calling it Jesusland. Well, anybody who's got a lick of sense and decency will take their jibe as a true compliment since although they don't believe it we know that Jesus is on our side and we appreciate it. It also goes to show that they really do admit that America is a Christian country.

Jews, The: The Chosen People—at least up until they killed Jesus. Still, they were there to set things up for Christianity so there's a real love/hate thing going on. Now that the Jews have their homeland back it's up to America to keep them there.

Jingoism: Patriotism on steroids.

Journalism: Journalism in the New American Century is simply taking press releases from corporations, the government, Wall Street and the Pentagon and putting them on the air waves and out in print. That is the correct way to disseminate information.

Investigative journalism is practiced by evil doing liberals who try to dig up dirt on our fine institutions. They are whistle-blowing traitors.

Judicial Appointments: In the New American Century there will be **no litmus test** for Judicial Appointments other than they be members of the Federalist Society, will pass the scrutiny of the "Rapture Right" and know the secret handshake.

Justice: A Heavenly Virtue that is built right into the American system because we have a Department of Justice. You can't get any more virtuous or heavenly than that! Justice in the New American Century will carry on just like it always has. (See Double Standard)

"Justice is incidental to law and order."

—J. Edgar Hoover (1895–1972)

"Justice is having and doing what is one's own."

—Plato (427-347 BC)

Justice, Department of: Having control of the executive gives the added bonus of being in control of the Justice Department where you get to set the agenda for going after who you want and looking the other way when you want.

Justice Sunday: Mayday, 2005—the faithful have raised a rallying cry and a challenge to the evildoers in Congress who would filibuster President Bush's most godly nominees to the bench. The use of the filibuster to thwart justice is an outrage! When Republicans did it to Clinton and forestalled up or down votes it was a matter of principle. That was different.

Just War: Thought to mean *Warranted* War, as in a Just War is a conflict that is necessary and is prosecuted in a just cause. Balderdash! As if America needs a justification for war! War is America's privilege and right. After all, it's just another war. Its just war for God's sake!

"War is peace. Freedom is slavery. Ignorance is strength."

—George Orwell (1903-1950)

"For all we have and are, For all our children's fate, Stand up and take the war. The Hun is at the gate!"

—Rudyard Kipling (1865-1936)

"War alone brings up to its highest tension all human energy and puts the stamp of nobility upon the peoples who have the courage to face it."

—Benito Mussolini (1883-1945)

K is for KILLING

KBR: Kellogg, Brown & Root, a subsidiary of Halliburton and yet another yankee doodle company ready, willing and able to help privatize America's military.

K Street Project, The: Started by Grover Norquist and Tom DeLay in 1995, the K Street Project has steadily bulked up the Republican side of lobbying firms while whittling down the ranks of Democrats in the influence peddling business. Since the Democrats will have no influence in the New American Century, it is only natural that they should be phased out. (See Lobbyist)

Kevorkian, Jack: Dr. Death, the infamous physician who helps people to commit suicide. Dr. Death looks like death warmed over and is really a weird character but he is also dangerous because if people are simply allowed to check out whenever they want it will adversely impact the intensive care industry.

Killing: One of the Ten Commandments is against wanton killing—that, of course, does not mean the killing of any enemy—real or perceived—of America. Internally, that also does not mean convicted murderers or, in Texas, thanks to the Futile Care Law, patients.

Kindness: One may show kindness to one's hunting dog or children less than seven years of age. Otherwise, kindness is a weakness.

King: America should have a King—a President King. After all, the Lord God is the King of the Universe and He runs things perfectly well with that form of government. If it's good enough for God it ought to be good enough for America. Of course, the King would have to be of the philosophy of the New American Century because we wouldn't want a tyrant.

KISS: Keep It Simple, Stupid. Long and rambling explanations tend to lose one's audience. You've got to grip them with a sound bite like "They hate us for our freedoms" or "They hate us because of Hollywood and its permissiveness."

Hit them quick and often and you'll have them repeating your particular mantra as if it were true. Explain the subtleties of a given situation and you will have them snoozing in the aisles. (See Sound Bites)

Kissinger, Henry Alfred (1923–): German born former Secretary of State and Assistant to the President for National Security Affairs and the sexiest man alive. Although not an architect of the New American Century, Kissinger certainly paved the way for its coming, especially in the area of secretive double dealings and covert operations.

KKK: Kinder, Kuchen und Kirche—children, cooking and church—the German equivalent to barefoot and in the kitchen for the good little hausfrau.

KKK, The: The Ku Klux Klan, a gentile southern organization founded in 1865 in order to defend the South from the ravages of northern scalawags and carpetbaggers. Originally, the KKK had a serious bone to pick with the post-Lincoln Republicans but now its membership is in solid with the GOP. It just goes to show you how strange politics is—the RNC once was the party of black folks and now they've jumped ship and foolishly hooked up with the Dems. There's plenty of room under the Big Tent for both groups, y'all. Even if you're black you can always come back.

Kuwait: A pipsqueak of a country on the southern border of Iraq that was intensely helpful in helping us have a reason to attack Iraq in the first place when it attacked Kuwait for slant-drilling and stealing its oil. America liberated Kuwait in Desert Storm so that its people could enjoy freedom under a dictatorial kingship.

L is for LIBERTY

Laissez-Faire: Another French term but not a sissified one. Laissez-faire means leave it alone to do its own thing. Specifically, this relates to government and business—namely for government to keeps its prying nose out of things and let the free market run its course. Of course, we all know that that could include the possibility of failure so Laissez-Faire economics is a bit too Libertarian for the New American Century taste bud. While we like to give a lot of tongue waggle to the free market we really need to be tweaking things behind the scenes to keep the profits high and our best buddies afloat. After all, impoverished campaign donors are about as useful as the proverbial lead balloon.

Land Mines: A truly horrible, sneaky weapon is the land mine. It also has the unfortunate side effect of staying dangerous for years endangering children, non-combatants and the very people who plant them. That's why America will never enter a treaty limiting land mines and is the world's number one exporter and distributor.

Land Reform: An insidious policy of foreign tyrants bent on distributing land to the undeserving. Any country that enacts land reform is a rogue state, a pariah and begs to be invaded and saved by civilized nations. Not many people are aware of this but Julius Caesar was killed by the Senate for attempting to institute land reform. More people should know it so they don't get any funny ideas.

Laughter: Laughter is the best medicine. The Pentagon actually has a Chief Laughter Instructor, James "Scotty" Scott to help the folks back home chase away the blues when they think of their loved ones overseas in harms way. That's a pretty good idea! Maybe every American should learn to laugh off whatever comes in the next phase of the New American Century.

Lawyers: There are good lawyers and bad lawyers. Good lawyers defend the ideals of the New American Century and corporate interests. Bad lawyers belong to the ACLU and support the defunct Democrat Party. One good thing about the bad lawyers, though, is that they are the butt of all those good lawyer jokes.

Leadership Institute, The: One of the premier training institutions of the New American Century and its ideals. Taking a two to four day seminar at the Institute qualifies you as an expert in any number of fields. James Dale Guckert, a.k.a. Jeff Gannon became a world-class journalist and member of the elite Washington Press Corps after only two days of instruction!

Liberal: What good can be said about people who are anti-freedom, anti-life, anti-business, freethinking, no-good upstarts? Everything in this whole wide world that is screwed up is a product of liberalism. There need be no proof of that—it's just so!

Liberals would have it that they are open-minded, fair and tolerant. Don't you believe a word of it! They are only open-minded, fair and tolerant for their own kind. All you really need to know about liberals is that they want big government to come in and control everything. Yeah, they're liberal about spending everyone else's money. That makes them think that they are modern Robin Hoods—taking from the rich and giving to the poor. What they want to do is destroy business and turn America into a communist hellhole.

Liberals would also have you believe that all the strides for the common man in America were liberal ideas—things like emancipation, women's suffrage, child labor laws, the 8-hour workday. There are many blacks, women, youths and workers who are Conservative and benefit from these things, too. So it's not all about liberals, is it? There you have it!

Liberals are never satisfied with the way things are so they always want to change everything. That is why Conservatives must dominate them and put things aright so that things can go back to the way they ought to have been.

Libertarians: Libertarians think they are the only true Conservatives and allow themselves a feeling of independence but will vote Republican anyway. Libertarians go way overboard in their views about getting government out of the public's face. They forget that Uncle Sam needs to keep an eye on them and everybody else. (See Useful Idiot)

Liberators: America is occupying Iraq as Liberators, much the same as Great Britain occupied Iraq as Liberators early in the last century.

Liberty: Liberty is granted to all Americans who toe the line. Like all freedoms, liberty has certain boundaries beyond which one must not stray. For example, one has the liberty to flail his arms about but one does not have the liberty to make contact with someone else's nose except in those cases where one actually does have the liberty to do so. Or, one cannot simply expose oneself to the opposite sex except at the appropriate time and place and with the consent of all parties involved. Or, one may not carry around and conceal dangerous firearms on their persons unless they have a permit. In short, one cannot go around doing just anything they please unless they have some sort of legal backing to do so. In fact, virtually all freedoms come with strings attached, except perhaps the freedom to be a failure. That you can be to your heart's content.

"Liberty exists in proportion to wholesome restraint."

—Danial Webster (1782-1852)

Limbaugh, Rush: Porcine god of truth and the sanctity of marriage in the New American Century. Mr. Limbaugh's status as the world's greatest entertainer and half-wit (claims to defeat his enemies with half of his brain tied behind his back) requires that his unfortunate addiction to OxyContin be considered a medical problem.

As leader and mind for all "dittoheads," Rush has not let his tremendous success go to his head. He remains the earthy, good old boy whose sole purpose in life is to uplift the common man as much as possible through the great engine of trickle down economic policies. Herewith are a few examples of his love for humanity and Mother Earth:

"Feminism was established to allow unattractive women easier access to the mainstream."

"The most beautiful thing about a tree is what you do with it after you cut it down."

"The NAACP should have riot rehearsals."

"If we are going to start rewarding no skills and stupid people—I'm serious, let the unskilled jobs, let the kinds of jobs that take absolutely no knowledge whatsoever to do—let stupid and unskilled Mexicans do that work."

Logic: The retreat of liberals, free thinkers and other such scoundrels.

Lobbyist: A person acting as a spokesman for a facet of corporate America doing extraordinarily important work in bringing important issues to the attention of government officials. Genuine lobbyists are not to be confused with extortionists for liberal causes such as the environment, gun control and consumer protection. Those are "special interests" and not true pork-barrel hounds that are so necessary to the American economy.

Thanks to the K Street Project and the ultimate Republican takeover of government, lobbying will become much simpler and direct in the New American Century. As laws become streamlined, the revolving door between legislators and jobs in top lobbying firms will become an open door, creating a wonderful fusion of corporate state power.

Loopholes: The law is like a diamond mine with many twists and turns, dark corners and labyrinthine pathways. Loopholes are the diamonds in the rough that the good lawyers (corporate lawyers) uncover in order to enrich their patrons.

Love: As the Greeks taught us, there are many kinds of Love; erotic Love being the "basest" and tough Love being the most pure. Tough Love gives one the fortitude to smack people around for their own good. Puppy Love is the next most pure kind of Love because it is so cute and innocent. Unconditional Love is ridiculous—and unnatural. Even God puts strings on his Love—you're either with Him or against Him. Heaven or Hell. That's the choice, baby! America does too: either Love it or leave it.

One may, as the Christians say, Love the sinner but hate the sin. This type of Love is reserved almost exclusively for homosexuals and is fostered in the hopes of eventually straightening them out. This type of Love is purely metaphorical. Sins other that homosexuality are simply not as venal and can therefore be made right with God. Thus, neither the sin needs to be hated nor the sinner to be loved.

Many people are confused into thinking that Love is the opposite of Hate as if the two were mutually exclusive. But don't you just Love to Hate liberal icons like Hanoi Jane or Jesse Jackson?

Lowering the Bar: Pretty much every standard set in the past is to be forgotten in favor of lowering the bar on expectations of quality and excellence. For example, in order to be more inclusive, the military will lower IQ standards so that many unfortunate unemployable youths can serve. And, of course, a Presidential speech need no longer be inspiring or uplifting. Rather, if delivered reasonably well—forget any content—then it will be considered a rousing success! As industry will be self-regulatory, product safety and quality will limbo down to tolerability and pharmaceuticals will sail through the FDA like a greased goose. Once public services are fully privatized one can expect cloudy water and brownouts. All in all, corporate profits will soar to new heights and progress will once again be on the march.

Lowest Common Denominator, The: Euphemism for striving toward the basest, meanest or poorest in quality as in universal laws regarding trade must necessarily be the weakest in terms of costs and environmental protection. In other words, the standard of the New American Century.

Lying: Telling little white lies in order to promote or protect the New American Century is not really lying at all. As they say, truth is stranger than fiction and who wants to engage in fiction, much less anything stranger than fiction? Thus, lying presents a more palatable view of things and is ultimately more acceptable.

Of course, you wouldn't want to—as President Bush says—*"disassemble"* (tell lies) about things that might have happened to you at Gitmo or Abu Ghraib. That is, for the detainees to not tell the truth about how they were treated and try to make America look bad. He made it clear that none of these charges was true and that America investigated every claim *against* the prisoners with the utmost of clarity. Those people that were held for a couple of years and then let go after being found to be innocent just had some kind of chip on their shoulder and can't be trusted. Any talk of maltreatment is just sour grapes.

Lynch, Jessica: Pvt. Jessica Lynch is a modern American heroine. Caught with her patrol by Iraqi insurgents, she went down both guns blazing despite multiple gunshot wounds, knife wounds and broken bones. All of her companions were killed but she survived only to be tortured and mercilessly interrogated until Army Rangers and Navy Seals staged a daring rescue and brought her back to freedom. Too bad most of the aforesaid was made up. (See Hollygon)

M is for MANDATE

Machiavelli, Niccolo (1469–1527): Italian statesman and philosopher, author of "The Prince," an inspiration to any politician.

MAD: Mutually Assured Destruction—the concept that fueled the arms race of the Cold War. In political circles, it is the gathering of incriminating evidence against one's own friends as a defense against one's own misdeeds coming to light. In order to cement the bonds of MAD there are a number of extremely private locations where one may "let one's hair down" in front of friends and gather useful information as well as voluntarily expose oneself as a gesture of good faith.

Madison Avenue: Home to the advertising industry. Of late, the home of campaign strategy and intimately linked to what might be called America's information ministry. Nowadays, you've got to sell the public on candidates and ideas and who better than advertising experts to handle the job?

Majority Report, The: Another one of those anti-American shows on Air America Radio hosted by Janeane Garofalo and Sam Seder. She likes to say bad things about the psychology of good Americans who support the New American Century while he just rants on and on about things that they, the lefties don't like. One cannot stress how utterly important it is that people tune in to another station during the Majority Report before their minds are overtaken with factual information. All you have to know is that President Bush is a Compassionate Conservative and he's doing all he can to protect you so you have to protect yourself from knowing anything else by never, ever listening to the Majority Report.

Malloy, Mike: They're everywhere—these Air America radio freaks! And believe you me; Mike Malloy is one of the freakiest of the bunch! He's a wild man. No matter which side you come down on Malloy will get your blood boiling. Just for the sake of your blood pressure you need to avoid listening to this guy!

Referring to the Bush Administration and anything smacking of the New American Century, Malloy asks, "Have I told you today how much I hate these people?" Well, Mike, I'm sure the feeling's mutual. You keep dwelling on things that people shouldn't concern themselves about like how hospitalized servicemen at Walter Reed and other military hospitals—injured in Iraq and Afghanistan—have to pay for phone calls and other services (like meals). You keep looking into the nooks and crannies where you shouldn't and just rile up folks when they should simply mind their own business and be content to know that whatever means are employed, the ends will justify them one way or the other. A traitor to the New American Century if ever there was one!

Mandate: Any electoral victory, no matter how slight the majority is a mandate for ushering in the New American Century. Should the opposition somehow win, it's clear that there can never be a mandate for their side because they must have cheated since the American people surely don't want to roll back any of the wonderful changes made during the last few years.

Manifest Destiny: The driving force of the Old American Century. It was America's Manifest Destiny to forge a nation from coast to coast. The New American Century is a glorious expansion of America's God given rights to global hegemony.

Marriage: The union between a man and a woman *only*, defined by God as a sacred bond that can be dissolved quite easily for any number of reasons. (Contrast with Covenant Marriage)

Mayberry Machiavellis: Former head of the President's faith based initiatives, John Dilulio's characterization of the Bush White House. In particular, he was referring to the control exerted by Karl Rove over all policy decisions. "What you got is everything, and I mean everything, being run by the political arm. It's the reign of the Mayberry Machiavellis," said he.

McClellan, Scott: The god of wind for the New American Century. In this age of horrific monster storms, Scott McClellan stands alone for sheer endurance in keeping the Washington Press Corps blown hither and yon, round and round, rambling in monotones in a great show of obfuscation. It's rumored that Scott got his job as Press Secretary for having asked "Are we there yet?" for over three hours straight on a family trip.

McWorld: A euphemism for the exporting of good old American know-how and efficiency.

Mean Spirited: Aw. Do the itty-bitty widdle gay loving, commie bastard, anti-American turds on the left feel like the Right is a bit nasty? Tough titties! What they can't take and call Mean Spirited is just tough love, telling it like it is and keeping it real. These crybabies need to be bitch-slapped into the real world where it's dog-eat-dog, screw your neighbor and I've got mine!

Means, The: Use any and all Means, for the Ends will justify them.

Media: There are two types of media in America: the liberal media and the Truth. The liberal media stands for anti-Americanism and it is the spawn of the Devil. The liberal media is everywhere, all pervasive, all perverting. One must forever be on guard against it. Fortunately, it is extremely easy to spot the liberal media as any media that does not proudly proclaim itself as coming from a Conservative and therefore, unbiased viewpoint. If, however, one has trouble finding the liberal media, one can locate two of their premier sources at Pacifica.org and Airamericaradio.com.

The New American Century will strive to stamp out the liberal media and any un-American voices in the homeland. Unfortunately, like the many-headed hydra the liberal media has the capacity to rebound from attempts at censorship. Witness the failed effort of Bob Dole in decrying Pacifica's KPFK (Los Angeles, 90.7 FM, 98.7 in Santa Barbara and streaming live on the web) as "hate radio". Viagra Bob's ill-timed rant had the undesired affect of nearly doubling KPFK's listener base.

For the brave-hearted who wish to tune in to the liberal media to see what is going on—be aware that it is a shocking adventure. One would think that one has stumbled upon a parallel universe where everything one knows to be good and wholesome has been turned on its head! The news of the day is presented as if our wonderful and fearless leaders are really not nice people! The great works that they do are twisted and represented as if they have ulterior motives that are not in the best interests of the people but instead tend to favor the rich and powerful to the detriment of the average person! It is absolutely mind-boggling how they skew the efforts of the World Bank, the IMF, the results of GATT and NAFTA and most of all, the Bush Administration. Why, if one were to believe even a tenth of what they are spewing then one might think that our most basic systems are being "gamed" in such a way as to favor a few instead of the many.

It's absolutely horrifying—a person cannot take but a few minutes of such nonsense without quickly tuning into Rush or Hannity or O'Reilly in order to be reassured that all is really hunky-dory and we are being protected 24/7 by those who have only our best interests at heart!

Medical Marijuana: We're in the middle of a Drug War and a bunch of sicko creeps want us to believe that marijuana relieves pain and stimulates the appetite more effectively than good old pharmaceuticals. Nice try, but what kind of a message would we be sending our children if we allowed the sick and dying to get loaded on illegal drugs? To alleviate their pain and suffering with an easy quick fix? There are plenty of high priced substitutes out there. Just because a person is sick it doesn't mean he or she can't still contribute to the economy.

Mercury: A.k.a. quicksilver, a highly toxic substance that has a nasty habit of getting into the ecosystem due to industrial processes. What are you going to do? Try not to ingest any. If you do, make sure you stay within the new guidelines.

Middle Class, The: The American Middle Class epitomizes the American Dream. The Middle Class lives in suburbia, having earned its way out of the city, rural poverty and farm drudgery. The Middle Class is the vast consumer class, enjoying luxuries unheard of in other countries. The Middle Class is the backbone of America and the New American Century is designed to crack that back like a wishbone, for it is evident that too many lowly citizens have been overpaid and pampered for far too long. Americans have grown fat and lazy in the machine age, falsely believing that mechanization is for relieving the heavier burdens of work rather than understanding its true value in increasing production. Now, we have to import most of our manufactured goods because Americans want high pay, benefits, holidays and all sorts of perks that they most certainly do not deserve. Well, the new normalcy will soon reveal that all this mollycoddling must come to a screeching halt. The Middle Class—whether you know it or not—you're on the endangered species list.

Miers, Harriet: The first groupie ever to be nominated by a President to the Supreme Court. Not since JFK tapped his own brother to be head of the Justice Department has there been a more audacious pick. No matter. The far right scuttled Harriet before she got out of the gate. No up or down for Harriet—just out!

Migrant Farm Workers: Beneficial human locusts that descend upon American farms, stripping them of their produce then go into hibernation until the next season.

Miller, Zell: Former *Democrat* Governor of Georgia (1990–1999) and now *Democrat* Georgia State Senator. Miller's address during the Republican National Convention earned him a spot as a minor deity in the New American Century—the god of indignation and bluster. Miller—madder than a wet hen or a tea party hatter—even went so far as to challenge reporter Chris Matthews to a duel because he was annoyed at the line of questioning. Well, Zell is definitely our kind of boy—ready to kick ass at the drop of a hat and as a Dixiecrat, a huge embarrassment to his party and himself.

Mission Accomplished: The lame-brained lefty naysayers and every other simpleton who thinks that President Bush's glorious proclamation aboard the USS Abraham Lincoln was a bit premature simply does not know what the mission was. After a few weeks of kicking Iraqi butt, America was able to get its corporate meathooks into that sorry country and begin pumping the resources out of it and into their coffers. That was and continues to be the mission.

Mistakes: The ability to make mistakes is a quality of people lacking in sufficient power to either ignore them or cover them up. Moreover, what may appear to be a mistake is simply a matter of perspective. One may attribute all sorts of errors to governmental policies that seemingly end in disaster but one person's disaster is assuredly another's opportunity. Therefore, it is a common mistake to think that one's betters have made mistakes. The general folly is, of course, from not being of sufficient height in order to view the Big Picture.

Misunderestimate: To improperly underestimate. If one does not underestimate to a low enough degree then one has misoverestimated one's *misunderestimate*.

Money: In addition to being cocaine encrusted promissory notes, money is also free speech. That is, money talks, bullshit walks and it is the medium used in buying politicians. Some call it filthy lucre and decry that the love of money is the root of all evil. That is total bunk. The root of all evil is Satan, as everyone knows.

"The universal regard for money is the one hopeful fact in our civilization. Money is the most important thing in the world. It represents health,

*strength, honour, generosity and beauty...Not the least of its virtues is that
it destroys base people as certainly as it fortifies and dignifies noble people."*

—George Bernard Shaw

Monopoly: The goal of any good company.

Moon, The Reverend Sun Myung: Remember the Moonies? Ah, well. Even
though the good Reverend is a bit eccentric, he is 100% on the side the New
American Century and deserves all the faith based funding America can give him.
His Holiness, the self-proclaimed second coming of Christ is a good friend of the
Bush family, even going so far as to retain the services of GHW Bush to help gain
a foothold in South America. His newspaper, the Washington Times is a bastion
of truth, honesty, fairness, family values and proper thought as befits an organ of
such an esteemed individual.

Moore, Michael: Michael Moron—a so-called documentarian who slams our
great President and the workings of the New American Century. Lately, he's been
trying to drum up a case against the Bush family and ties to the Saudi royal family and their friends, the Bin Ladens. First they claimed that President Bush
didn't know anything about the outside world and now they are complaining
that he knows real people who actually don't live in America. Moore and his ilk
just can't stand that successful people like each other.

More Study: If it appears that there is a groundswell amongst the populace to
enact legislation that may be against the goals of the New American Century it is
prudent to call for more study of the situation. Virtually anything can thus be
stalled, for as new evidence comes in one can always count on paid experts to
refute said evidence and muddy the waters—calling for more study to determine
what must be done.

Moral Compass: One's innate sense of morality. If one's Moral Compass is not
always pointed toward the direction of the New American Century then one is
lost.

Motives: People have underlying reasons for everything they do. Regardless of
the circumstance, it is imperative to project a moral root cause for everything that
good Americans do. For example, despite all of the unfounded reasons for taking
over Iraq, we remain steadfast in the noble cause of freeing the Iraqi people and

bringing democracy to the Middle East. A liberal, on the other hand, will save a drowning woman only because he hopes she will be grateful enough to have sex with him.

Mythology: Superstition and mythology have always been with us—created out of the mind of man in order to explain the world and at the same time, to cover it with fanciful tales that we wish were true.

Consider with what disdain Messers Heinrich Kramer and James Sprenger looked upon the ancients with their classical mythological tales of the Olympian gods. To be sure, these two—a pair of the most learned men of the 15th century—revered the classical Greeks for their art, their literature, their philosophies and architecture but they must have scoffed at the notion of a pantheon of gods as mere silliness and a demonstration of Satanic influence.

These two gentlemen wrote the *Malleus Maleficarum* (the Witches' Hammer) in all earnestness as a manual to witch hunters of the day. And for nearly three centuries it was the definitive guide for finding, exposing and ridding the countryside of demonic forces. Included are the modus operandi of succubi, incubi, demons and devils. In considerable detail they argue all manner of ways in which evil beings interface with mankind. For example, they examine whether or not devils can impregnate women. Question IX of Part One asks, "Whether witches may work some prestidigitatory illusion so that the male organ appears to be entirely removed and separated from the body." And there is much, much more, written without a shred of insincerity; for these scholars absolutely believed in everything they said and they were the penultimate experts in their field. Due to their zeal and the enthusiasm of others it is estimated that upward of *seven million* women were killed in Europe during those times. This was a grim business with the good people defending themselves against unspeakable evil.

Now, if it weren't so tragic we might be disposed to laugh at such nonsense—we the enlightened people of the modern scientific era—but not so fast. The truth is that contemporary man is still the scared little creature who cannot face the world as it truly is and thus surrounds himself in notions that he so fervently wishes to be the truth. We cleave to the absolute "truth" of our scientific method. We continue to do outrageous things to "others" because we are secure and comforted with the knowledge that we are the good and that *our* deity blesses and condones our behavior. Like our forbears, we see evildoers everywhere.

Hitler tried to create a mythic heroic image of the Teutonic superman—superior, strict, self-controlled, efficient—and succeeded to a large degree. The New American Century will use democratic idealism, zealous patriotism and uncompromising religion to forge a presumably greater destiny for mankind. We are without a doubt at the onset of a great mythic age.

N is for NATIONAL SECURITY

Nac: Short for New American Century—a new slang word to replace the slang word "cool" when affirming some positive person, thought, word or deed associated with the New American Century. The 2000 World Almanac listed the 10 most influential people of the 2nd millennium: Shakespeare, Newton, Darwin, Copernicus, Galileo, Einstein, Columbus, Lincoln, Gutenburg and William Harvey. It's interesting to note that of this list, eight are definitely nac. One is cool (Shakespeare) and Darwin is most definitely not nac *and* not cool.

While it is still cool to listen to jazz, it is not cool to watch smart bombs doing their thing. It is nac, baby! Hostile takeovers, technology, Jesus, anything military—these are all nac. Bush, Cheney—the whole gang—they're all nac. Having a baby is cool as long as it was planned for and has all its fingers and toes. Knowing someone of another ethnic group is also cool.

Napalm: A really hideous weapon that does a wonderful job. America doesn't use napalm anymore. It uses incendiary devices. (See White Phosphorous)

NASA: Formerly, America' space exploration agency. In the New American Century it will be America's space *exploitation* agency and the medium for the militarization of the heavens. Being the most generous people on earth, the American people will gladly bear the cost and heavy lifting of space flight and quickly allow for the privatization of any facet that proves profitable to industry. NASA's ultimate goal will be to put powerful space based laser weaponry in geosychronous orbit about the planet so that if anything suspicious shows its face on the surface, it will be toast. Rather than having a "red button" at the White House, the President will soon have a red joystick.

Nascar: The best sport in many ways. One, it can be far more deadly than any other. Two, there's no rubbing or tackling or any other kind of man grabbing going on. Three, no liberals allowed. Four, it has the greatest concentration of advertising known to man. Five, noise and air pollution levels are not controlled by the EPA.

National Identification Card: Although we already have a national ID number, i.e., the social security number, now we are about to get hooked up with a National Identification Card that will be chipped so they can track us all a little better. Maybe Big Brother can't count the hairs on your head yet but he can certainly find out what you're buying, when and where and he will certainly be interested in how you're paying and why you want it.

National Security: Protecting military, governmental and corporate assets worldwide. In addition, National Security is a justification for all manner of clandestine actions and invoking it trumps snooping snoopers from discovering what's going on. The only chink in the armor of National Security is the Whistle-blower, the vilest form of tattletale.

Nationalism: The world is being "Balkanized" by nationalistic spirit. This sort of regional jingoism is not healthy because along with each government you have to set up trade relations, have separate negotiations and on and on. Its so much easier dealing with one central power that doesn't care much for its nether regions. Besides, what do these people have to be nationalistic about? They aren't Americans.

Nation Building: The world is a mess and it's up to America to set things right. No longer the world's policeman, America must assume the role as the world's carpenter and founding father.

Native Americans: Indigenous pre-Columbian natives to the American continent that stood in the way of Manifest Destiny and had to be removed. Native Americans are enjoying a comeback in the casino business and are also handy in lending names to sports teams and school mascots.

Nazi: Everyone knows that the Nazis lost World War II whereupon all the fanatics disbursed and totally renounced the philosophy of fascism, embracing democratic ideals and became model citizens of the world. There are no more Nazis in the world today. Don't go looking for any because they just don't exist anymore. It was all Hitler's fault and he's dead.

Negroponte, John: America's first Director of National Intelligence—the guy that heads up all the spooks, narcs and spies. Negroponte was the Ambassador to

Honduras during the Iran-Contra era and recently has served as Ambassador to Iraq (despite the fact that there really is no Iraq at present). His service in and around shady doings makes him an excellent choice for being the man in charge of telling the President what he wants to hear.

Neo-Con: Short for neo-conservative, a new type of conservative. Neo-cons are bold, outgoing, adventurous and totally behind the New American Century. In fact, the Neo-Cons belong to the Project for a New American Century (PNAC), the think tank that invented the New American Century. Old conservatives (paleo-cons) are the downbeat Nixonian types who still believe in small government and individual rights. Nonetheless, paleo-cons can be expected to vote Republican in the pitiful hope that the party will return to the old ideals.

Nepotism: Family values for business. Man's inalienable right to advance relatives over non-relatives, friends over non-friends and lovers over non-lovers.

New Normalcy, The: Life in the New American Century. The public is just going to have to get used to it. Of course, the New Normalcy is anything but new or even normal since things will be changing fairly rapidly, adjusting to the inevitable bumps and grinds as things shift into new patterns.

News: Formerly, no news was good news. In the New American Century news is one of the greatest diversionary tactics. There is always a scandal involving some celebrity or a sensational murder that can be highlighted so as to divert the attention of the masses. In a pinch, news can be totally invented.

New World Order, The: The old term that anticipated the New American Century. Since America is going to be running things, the world order is going to be American.

NGO: Non-governmental organization. Liberal NGO's are groups concerned with causes that are unimportant to governments but still manage to insinuate themselves into meetings between countries.

NIMBY: Not In My Back Yard. Nobody wants a dangerous, polluting, stinking factory or prison where they live so everybody invokes NIMBY. NIMBY only works where there is political strength, however, so you can be sure that that factory or jail is going to be built somewhere.

911 Commission, The: The New American Century's first successful white-wash. Now that FOIA has revealed that the government had at least 52 warnings related to the incident, it may be necessary to implement round 2 of the white-wash. However, for the time being it seems that simply ignoring the findings and keeping it off the front pages is having the desirable effect of having the whole matter become lost in the swamplands of the distant past.

Nixon, Richard M. (1913–1994): The 37th President. A tragic figure in American history, Richard Nixon had the bad luck to be President in an era when the people cared if the government was corrupt. Honored as being the President who ended the Vietnam War after having extended it five years, his greatest flaw was in not having erased his memoir tapes. (See Appendix E)

No Child Left Behind: Having worked diligently for years to undermine the public school system, it is necessary and most expedient to introduce a new scam on the public to replace the old ways. This one is a stroke of pure genius for it is a huge boon to publishing companies as textbooks must be revised and more importantly, a vast array of testing material must be created and bought at public expense. While analyzing America's youth, the results can (and will) be used to evaluate their potential as future factory drudges, cannon fodder (if schools want the federal bucks they have to fork over names, addresses and phone numbers of recruitment age kids) or meat for the prison industrial complex. Furthermore, pharmaceuticals can get in on the action, as corrective drugs will be legislated to be administered to certain types. This is a strategy that has a big payoff for years to come!

Norquist, Grover: A true player in the New American Century. This board member of the NRA and the American Conservative Union helped GW slime John McCain in the South Carolina primary. No slouch in the spinmeister department, Norquist also helps get out the talking points to all the Conservative pundits. He knows what he wants and isn't afraid to say it: "My goal is to cut government in half in twenty-five years, to get it down to the size where we can drown it in the bathtub." Keep it up Grover and your 25-year prediction will be seen to have been a bit too conservative.

North Korea: The third leg of the trio, the Axis of Evil. North Korea has been a sore spot ever since it came into being in 1953. Currently, it is under the leadership of crazed tyrant and head pygmy Kim Jong Il, whose penchant for hot babes, Hollywood and fine dining only goes to show that no matter what type of society you live in, if you're top dog you get the treats.

The whole Korea thing is hugely troublesome for America. Unifying the two Koreas would surely aid in world stability but it would also bring into being yet another Asian super producer that would be a formidable economic engine. Keeping North Korea bottled up is killing off the peasantry and pressuring an already over-bloated military, which may or may not have *nucular* weaponry. Throw China and Japan into the mix and you've got some real headaches brewing.

Non-Security Discretionary Spending: In America's budget, there is military spending, security spending and Non-Security Discretionary Spending, the latter being everything that is really needed to run a country. In the New American Century, such spending is to be kept at a minimum because in an Ownership Society everyone can take care of his or her self and doesn't need any government handouts and the like with the exception of faith-based charities.

NORAD: North American Aerospace Defense Command. Despite having scrambled jets 67 times in the year prior to 9/11/2001, it was apparently not enough practice to deal with the main event.

Novus Ordo Saeculorum: Old Italian for "a new order of ages"—a New World Order. It's right there on your dollar bill. Right under the all-seeing eye!

NRA, The: Politically, it is expedient to court this, one of the largest and most powerful public interest groups in America and uphold gun rights to the extreme. Realistically, allowing any sort of riff-raff weaponry is a threat to the oligarchy and an impediment to removing all resistance of the populace to total control. In due time we shall revisit all gun control laws. For now fortunately, the NRA's blind loyalty to the Conservative cause has thus far lulled them into compliance with the ultimate goals of the New American Century. (See Useful Idiots)

NSA, The: The National Security Agency—while the CIA gets all the glamour, this is really the granddaddy of all of the spooks. In the New American Century, **NSA** stands for **N**owadays **S**noops on **A**mericans.

Nucular **Energy**: A really spiffy, hi-tech way to make America energy independent and provide as many *nucular* bombs and depleted uranium weapons as we want.

Nucular **Option**: No, it doesn't have anything to do with a red phone or pushing buttons and blowing up the world. This is just a name somebody made up for ending the Democrat's ability to filibuster a judicial nominee that would be kind of like blowing up the opposition to any fine, upstanding, moral, law-abiding, peach of a guy who will uphold the tenets of the New American Century, the Ten Commandments and interpret existing laws to fit the plan.

Nucular **Proliferation**: Not good. America is the only country that can be trusted to use *nucular* weapons responsibly. Nevertheless, there's a whopping lot of money to be made selling dual use technology and the like.

O is for OIL

Occupation: The placing of American troops in a foreign country in order to liberate the local inhabitants and place them under martial law.

OIL: Operation Iraqi Liberation—the code name for the invasion of Iraq until someone pointed out the obvious. Changed to Operation Iraqi Freedom, OIF.

Oil: Manna from the Underworld that greases the skids and fuels the engines of the worldwide economy. That is, Black Gold, Texas Tea. Unfortunately, most of our cheap, clean and easily accessible oil is under the Middle East.

Oil Executives: Gods of Power and Self Destruction in all the ages of internal combustion. These formidable beings are the uberlords of modern society, operating in a lofty realm so far exceeding mankind that they are above reproach, above all standards, above the law. Their word is the law—not to be questioned or sullied by oaths.

Oil for Food Program: In order not to entirely starve off the Iraqi people while we kept Saddam bottled up it was necessary to set up the Oil for Food Program that allowed countries to buy Iraqi oil for humanitarian aid and foodstuffs. Unfortunately, this program turned out to be completely corrupted not only by Saddam but by certain elements of the UN and maybe a little more than half of the illegal doings were under the auspices of a few Texas corporations but that in no way absolves the UN for being entirely at fault!

Oligarchy: The real way America is governed.

> *"Where some people are very wealthy and others have nothing, the result will be either extreme democracy or absolute oligarchy, or despotism will come from either of those excesses."*
>
> —Aristotle

Opium: Made from poppies, this illegal drug was floundering in Afghanistan under the Taliban rule. Now that America has liberated the country, Yankee know-how has put the opium trade back on track and production is booming.

O'Reilly, Bill: The New American Century's god of tough talk and vicarious living. If it's got to do with guts, glory, grit and porn then O'Reilly's been there and done that even if it's only his in own mind. You can count on this righteously indignant pundit to stop any liberal in his tracks by screaming "SHUT UP!"—a tactic that just keeps on making him one of the fiery and unbalanced debate champs of the airwaves.

Orthodoxy: Behaving in a fashion commensurate with the New American Century.

Orwell, George (1903–1950): Author of *Animal Farm* and *1984*, both tremendously useful novels in providing blueprints for social change necessary for the New American Century and the introduction of "newspeak," the terminology of the New American Century. Orwell's insightful works are to be publicly maligned as the ravings of a paranoid but they should privately be studied and farmed for new ideas on how to control Joe Six Pack.

Outsourcing: The way in which corporate America bestows its largess upon foreign populations by providing employment to the teeming masses of the third world. At the same time, outsourcing stimulates American workers to reject unionism and seek employment in new sectors to better themselves. The downside of outsourcing is that there are a number of jobs that simply cannot be sent overseas and it is up to immigration to help in this regard.

Oversight: In the New American Century, Oversight will consist of keeping tabs on any liberality that might be creeping into the legislation. Also, they'll be a weather eye out for anybody that has any criticism or worse yet, anyone who has the audacity to point out any irregularity in the works. They will be promptly taken care of!

Overtime: While it is cheaper to work a few people over and pay them overtime pay than to hire more people, it's still cheaper to work them over and either pay them regular time or have them work off the clock. Congress has stuck its nose in business' business by enacting the FairPay Law which mandates overtime pay for hourly workers making $455/week or less. While that means a few million of the exploited will be less exploited, the new law opens loopholes that business can use to scale down some of the overpaid middle class!

Ownership Society: The New American Century is ushering in a new society for America—the Ownership Society—highlighted by responsibility, liberty and prosperity. From now on Americans will be free from big government and entitlements to be secure in the bosom of the free market by taking responsibility for their own health care, retirement, insurance, etc., having the liberty to neglect all of the aforesaid and enjoying prosperity by being prosperous. Just Buy It!

OxyContin: A narcotic drug approved for the treatment of moderate to severe pain, especially the pain of having to constantly decry the outlandish misadventures of liberals.

Oxymoron: An obvious pun would be to say that an oxymoron is some highly touted though incredibly insincere and fatuous person who abuses OxyContin but we shall not stoop to such levels here. An oxymoron is an incongruous grouping of words that seem to contradict one another as in *giant shrimp* or *liberal Conservative*. Currently, there is a big brouhaha over the British admitting that there were high-level talks between Bush and Blair as well as their home-boys as to how to "sex up" the case against Saddam well before Congress or the House of Lords were informed. To date, the Bushies have remained quiet about these revelations. Oxymoron-ically, their silence is deafening.

P is for PATRIOTISM

Pacifica Radio Foundation: Here is a super liberal network of radio stations that will never make it. This bunch of lefty stations is wholly listener sponsored—they don't have commercials! This will never work—programming that goes far beyond the six-minute attention span of the average American. Imagine hearing entire uncut speeches, lectures and forums on subjects ranging from local issues to worldwide concerns, from spirituality to automotive repair, obscure music to health and healing and much, much more. Boring! And their affiliates (KPFA, San Francisco, KPFK, Los Angeles, KPFT, Houston, WBAI, New York, WPFW, Washington, D.C.) have their own local steering committees that decide programming *democratically*! Even if Pacifica has been broadcasting for over 50 years, it'll never work. (See www.pacifica.org/)

Pacifists: Anti-war wimps that won't defend themselves because they suffer from some sort of mental illness. Pacifists want to pretend that there aren't evildoers everywhere that want to do America harm and are just waiting for the right moment to pounce all over us. They live in this fantasy world where people can get along. How can anybody be so naïve?! It's all about them wanting to kill us because we're free or they're jealous of what we've got and they want to take it away from us. Don't these people realize that there are *millions* of foreigners in America right now! Right in our own midst! And there are home grown nutcases: fellow travelers, bomb throwing anarchists, all sorts of peace freak radicals and pacifists, too. They're all out to get us! They're crazy!

Palestine: A made up place that never existed except as a Roman colony named by Hadrian. The indigenous people have no more right to a homeland than anybody else who wants to just squat and claim they have a country.

Paper Trail: While it is necessary to have documentation of all sorts of things it is often more desirable to leave things out of print and just have certain gentleman's agreements simply because there are always evildoers who will misconstrue and misrepresent one's goals and dealings. And, of course, there are many trans-actions that just do not need to be memorialized. Voting is one example.

Pardons: Pardons are wonderful powers given to elected officials ostensibly to right wrongs done to people who used questionable methods to do the right thing or those who were railroaded into prison by un-American extremists. In lib-eral hands, it is used to excuse criminal behavior.

Patriot Act, The: A mishmash of laws and parts of laws and revisions to laws and revisions to parts of laws that good Americans need not bother their heads about. The good Americans in the House and Senate didn't, so why should anyone else? All the Patriot Act does is remove obstacles from law enforcement officers so they don't have to bother busy judges with niggling details. Too much noise has been raised over "loss of rights". Those who protest the Patriot Act simply are not patriotic and should be more closely watched. Patriot Act II will see to that.

Patriotism: It has been called the last refuge of scoundrels but it is also the first refuge of the quick thinking as it provides such a wonderful shield. Remember, the Means justify the Ends and if the Ends are linked to Patriotism, well then it's Katie bar the door!

> *"Patriotism is your conviction that this country is superior to all other coun-tries because you were born in it."*
> —George Bernard Shaw (1856–1950)

> *"Patriotism is the willingness to kill and be killed for trivial reasons."*
> —Bertrand Russell (1872–1970)

Pax Americana: The gift to the world that America has to offer. Everybody in the bosom of Lady Liberty is secure knowing that America is calling the shots and protects them from the barbarians within and without the gates.

Peacenik: A yellow commie out to kill good Americans.

Peacetime: That uneasy period between wars when the citizenry starts getting used to the idea of having no conflicts. Peacetime is best spent building up and increasing military spending while keeping the peasantry in constant terror of impending war. If this is not possible, money can still be made selling arms to belligerent nations, right-wing counter-insurgencies, death squads and future foes everywhere.

Pension Funds: Ostensibly set up as retirement funds for employees, these slush funds are available to be raided by corporations as a hedge against big fines, low dividends or simple bankruptcy.

Pentagon, The: One of the Corridors of American Power. Its unique shape signifies the five wonders it bestows on American life: service contracts, arms contracts, as a revolving door training center for industry, as an unquestioned secrecy umbrella for national security and for the projection of power worldwide. There are as well five great precepts of the Pentagon: hear no evil, see no evil, speak no evil, don't ask and don't tell.

Pharmaceutical Companies: For the most part, pharmaceutical companies are rigorously engaged in finding new ways to apply old drugs and buying millions of dollars of advertising in order to convince the public they need them.

Plame, Valerie: "Outed" CIA agent and wife of Joseph Wilson who reported that Saddam Hussein was not buying yellow cake uranium from Niger. Although letting out the secret that Ms. Plame was an agent is a federal crime and a breach of national security, it was important to do it in order to school others that bringing contrary news to the Bush Administration can have negative results.

Plausible Denial: No matter how unlikely an alibi is it is to be touted as that which has actually transpired. Plausible denial is the comforter on the bed of politics.

Plutocrats: The lofty persons who make up the Oligarchy.

PNAC: The Project for a New American Century. A think tank whose long ranging plans leads one to believe that they should have been called the Project for a New American Millennium, as it will surely create an empire to last for a thousand years! The core of its philosophy is to strengthen America militarily and project power over the world for the greater glory of Israel.

In a famous letter written by PNAC the course of American foreign policy was spelled out in intricate detail. Since many of the signatories are now members of the current administration, it appears that this document is indeed our foreign policy blueprint.

Police, The: Totally ill funded, under educated and outnumbered in today's America. That's why we need to pass laws allowing the National Guard and the Army to help out in the law enforcement business.

Police State: Well, that's a bit of a harsh term. Nevertheless, once the New American Century gets under full swing it will be something of a necessity in order to protect the populace from its tendencies. Indeed, the police are there to protect and serve. So a Police State merely protects and serves. Won't that be nice?

Politically Correct: Political Correctness *had* a dampening effect on free speech, especially the right to be as rude and obnoxious as possible. For a time, the wussy crybaby liberals were able to get folks to stop telling the truth about each other but those days are long gone and the tables have been turned by taking political correctness to absurd levels and making a mockery of the concept. An example of belittling PC would be in applying it to the past as in, "What if Homer had to be politically correct? Can you imagine the Cyclops after being poked in the eye by a sharp burning log jumping up and screaming, 'I'm visually challenged! I'm visually challenged!'" Such imagery is not only mirthful but it shows how out of control PC can get.

Nowadays, folks go out of their way so as *not* to be politically correct by being just as offensive as they feel they have a right to be. Of course, if a liberal is a little too candid it is up to everyone to remind him that his comments are out of bounds and cannot be tolerated.

Politics: Ah, the inscrutable Chinese! Leave it to them to best sum up what the New American Century is all about. Many thanks to the late, great Joseph Campbell for digging up these telling lines from *Shang Tzu* (Oriental Mythology, Penguin Books USA, Inc., 1962, p 409-410).

"If a country is strong and does not make war there will be villainy within and the Six Maggots, which are, to whit: rites and music, poetry and history; the cultivation of goodness, filial piety and respect for elders; sincerity and truth; purity and integrity; kindness and morality; detraction of warfare and shame at taking part in it. In a country that has these twelve things, the ruler will not be able to make people farm and fight, with the result that he will become impoverished and his territory diminished."

We are also told that, "A country where the virtuous govern the wicked will suffer from disorder, so that it will be dismembered; but a country where the wicked govern the virtuous will be orderly, so that it will become strong…"

And as for honorable behavior: "If things are done that the enemy would be ashamed to do, there is an advantage."

Polling: Polling is ostensibly the taking of a completely random sample of people and gathering information from them in order to see certain trends in public opinion, habits, preferences, etc. However, polling is really an art wherein the artist (polling company) paints a pleasing picture (obtains a pre-determined result) by a careful blend of style (by asking leading questions) and substance (by targeting a certain population).

Pop Culture: Satan's work here on earth. Pop Culture is the antithesis of family values. It's the glitz and glamorous lifestyle that lures the boys off the farm and makes daddy's little girl a painted whore. Pop Culture resounds with ethnic rhythms, bright lights and late nights, movie stars and shady underworld characters. It's the fast track to Hell for the decadent, the perverted, the shameless and the high rollers. It's American and the rest of the world envies the hell out of it.

Population: The world's comfortable carrying capacity is probably really around ½ billion. That would provide more than adequate working class folks to support the wealthy. With the population at around 6 billion currently and projected to rise to 9 billion by the middle of the century it is high time we had a nice epidemic, *nucular* war or tremendous natural catastrophe.

Pork: From Pork Barrel. Pork is that which one receives in the way of government contracts or out and out subsidies for having greased the palms of politicians. Without pork the feeding trough of government handouts would dry up and blow away—and so would the support of many a fearless leader.

Posse Comitatus: Enacted in 1878, Posse Comitatus is thought to be a stopgap against allowing the military to be involved in law enforcement inside of America except in times of national emergency. Forget about it. We've been using military to interdict drugs for years. It's just a silly fine point in the law that will almost certainly be forgotten in the New American Century.

POTUS: President of the United States. The big guy. The man in charge. America's CEO and Commander in Chief. The mealy mouthed democrats on the judicial committee tried to get Samuel Alito to say that he believed that the POTUS was above the law. This great man did not succumb to their foul baiting. He made that perfectly clear that no one is above the law—the POTUS *is* the law.

Power: One of the twin pillars of that which makes life meaningful—the other, of course, being wealth. Power translates wealth into action. Properly used, power creates more wealth and in turn, more power. It has been said that power corrupts and absolute power corrupts absolutely. This cliché was coigned by some powerless, jealous loser. Besides, as God is all-powerful the implication is blasphemous!

Pragmatism: That down to earth, no-nonsense, keeping-it-real philosophy of every good Conservative. Liberals are fuzzy-headed idealists and wishful thinkers, unable to give (or even understand) tough love because they lack the grit of pragmatic thinking. A peace freak, for example, will tell you that American companies shouldn't make land mines but since somebody has to make them it might as well be us. That's pragmatism.

Preamble to the Constitution, The: "We the People of the United States, in Order to form a more perfect Union, establish Justice, insure domestic Tranquility, provide for the common defence, promote the general Welfare, and secure the Blessings of Liberty to ourselves and our Posterity, do ordain and establish this Constitution for the United States of America." That's all well and good—and perhaps a bit quaint—but it's in God we trust and to the flag we pledge our allegiance.

Predatory Lending: You can't just allow anyone to lend money to certain groups in order to create permanent debt slavery unless you are a credit card company.

Preemptive War: America can't be caught sleeping at the switch again so it's high time we adopt a new policy toward making war—that being, if we so much as suspect anyone cowardly enough to sucker punch America then we have every right to hit them first and hit them hard! Fortunately, countries powerful enough to hit back don't go around behind someone's back so we really don't have to worry about them going for any sneak attacks and with them we can use diplomacy. That's the prudent thing to do.

Pre-Nuptial Agreement: A hedge against your bet that you can make a sacred vow permanent.

Pride: Yet another of the original Seven Deadly Sins that has outlived its usefulness. There is nothing wrong with Pride. One should be proud to be an American or, if an alien, proud to want to be an American. Taking pride in something un-American—now *that* goeth before a fall!

Prison Industrial Complex, The: Who would have thought that people could make so much money off of incarcerating others? With all of the wars on everything we've got going there's reason enough to put practically everybody in jail.

Privacy: In the new American Century the right to privacy is sacrosanct except in those cases where it isn't. Better put, you have the right to privacy wherever you can pay for it.

Privatization: Privatization of public services into the private sector has been proceeding at full clip and will continue to do so in the New American Century. Once the government has been stripped bare, selling its assets for a dime on the dollar and corporate America has taken over all vital functions it will mean the end of wasteful spending on public services—that is, the end of *all* spending on public services. Of course, if a business fails the government must be prepared to rush back in and buy back the industry at a handsome profit to the bosses who ran it into the ground. That the New American incentive package!

Profiling: If it looks like a duck…If a certain group of troublemakers doesn't like profiling then they should clean up their act! Think about it. Who are the people who perpetrate the most crimes in America? Shouldn't they be singled out, hauled over, patted down, strip searched, followed and generally harassed for their aberrant behavior? That would be nice but there are just too many white people who look like each other and it would be too much of a hassle to bother them. The police and law enforcement agencies have their hands full just looking after all the minorities as it is!

Pro-Life Movement, The: America's tenderhearted pre-baby lovers are wonderful because you can count on them to vote for pro-NAC (New American Century) candidates. They thoroughly support American military adventures and tend to ignore environmental degradation directly impacting prenatal health. Their silly detractors, those in the Anti-Life Movement try to disparage these fine folks by calling them Anti-Choice. This is a preposterous appellation since they obviously chose to be Pro-Life, a choice in and of itself.

Product Liability: A heinous and outmoded drain on profitability is the concept of product liability wherein a manufacturer is liable for the safety of its products. Fortunately, farsighted and patriotic legislators in the New American Century are reversing these restrictive laws and allowing the public greater freedom and lowered costs by virtue of removing silly, expensive safeguards and warning labels.

Progress: It is imperative that Progress be always on the march. It appears that we will always be having technological Progress—and that's good. That is at least one thing we can count on and boast about. But have we made Progress in the democratization and liberation of Iraq? Some would say no, but these would be the nattering nabobs of negativity doing the nay saying. Progress is a matter of semantics and if you were a board member of Halliburton or Bechtel Corp. you would probably feel that a whole lot of Progress has been made on the war front. So, as with beauty, Progress is in the eye of the beholder.

Progressive: The liberals are running scared from the "L" word and are now calling themselves Progressives. What does that make Conservatives? Regressives?

Progressive Taxation: Of all forms of taxation, this is the worst because it unfairly burdens the wealthy. Progressive is another word for liberal. Liberal is another word for bad. Bad is another word for demonic. Therefore, Progressive Taxation is Demonic Taxation.

Promotion: Getting ahead in the New American Century can be accomplished in many ways. One sure way is to fail upward. Our beloved POTUS is a fine example of such a tactic.

Proof: If a faithful follower of Conservatism makes an assertion, requiring proof is completely unnecessary and in some cases, downright unpatriotic. If, on the other hand, demonic life-hating liberals make a case against the New American Century, it simply proves that they are lying.

With regards to proving a person's guilt there are naturally varying circumstances. If a "warrior" for the New American Century is put to trial then it must be shown without a shadow of a smidgeon of a scintilla of a doubt that this person was guilty of any charges brought forward. Now as for others—black people, for example—if put to trial but not guilty of the charge at hand, it is more than likely that they are guilty of something they've gotten away with in the past. Therefore, they're guilty of something and that's good enough to satisfy American justice.

Propaganda: Propaganda is such an unseemly foreign sounding word. In fact, only nasty foreign regimes use propaganda. When it comes to promoting the best in Americanism (the ideals of the New American Century), the American government uses open, forthright non-coercive means, namely slick empty sound bites, paid newsmen and constant repetition. Doing so is not only right but it is the obligation of the government to influence the citizenry. (See Public Relations)

Proportional Democracy: A terrible idea that would make all of the states purple with some states being purpler than others. As well, it would make election rigging harder and even perhaps fruitless since it only really works well where the people are convinced that there is a close race.

Prosperity: When speaking to the public at large, the word Prosperity is not to be used. In the New American Century, Prosperity is reserved for industry and its owners. The commons must be told that the American economy is in perpetual Recovery, that the sacrifices that they must make are helping America out of the doldrums (although the Economy is robust and doing just fine). In that way, they will accept evermore cuts in social spending, stagnant wages, rotting infrastructure and the like but will remain optimistic about some future that will never be theirs.

Prudent: The no-wimp manly word for caution, used extensively by former President GWH Bush, one of our manliest and most forceful presidents. Prudence is one of the Seven Heavenly Virtues but really, how are you going to grab the gusto if you hold back?

PTSD: Post Traumatic Stress Disorder—shell shock. Anyone who goes crazy during war has to have been crazy in the first place and they should all be lined up and slapped. Certainly, they don't deserve wasting good old tax dollars on medical care.

Public Opinion: What the people long for may or may not be a part of the agenda. When it goes against the plan, ignore it and claim you have made your choice out of consistency, duty and moral sense—not to win a popularity contest. When the public is with you, ride their enthusiasm like a surfer on the perfect wave.

Public Relations: The art of convincing the public what to like, what to dislike, how much and when in total disregard of their own best interests. The spawn of Advertising.

Public Servant: Any Conservative who sacrifices his personal life for the good of the country doing government work advancing the New American Century. Should a kindly corporation hire this noble person after doing his civic duty that would be wonderful! Liberals claim that they are public servants as well but they are in it just for the job and the perks and because they can't make it in the real world.

Public Speaking: The art of stringing together banalities and buzz words in such a way as to spellbind a crowd of sycophants.

Push Poll: Not a legitimate poll but one hell of a good way to smear someone. Push polls are really telephone canvassing wherein the caller pretends to be taking a poll but the questions are such that they tend to smear or give outright false information about a particular candidate or group. Push polls are pretty effective because the fish on the line is so flattered to being polled he or she believes it's on the up and up and will swallow the bait.

Q is for QUID PRO QUO

Quack: Anyone with whom the AMA disapproves, regardless of their ability to heal.

Quagmire: Something we're not in and even if we were it would be because of freedom hating insurgents bent on opposing a just occupation and the rule of American law.

Quaint: Ideas or notions that once had great import but just don't seem to matter any more—like the Geneva Convention.

Qualifier: A qualifier is a phrase tacked onto a declaration that renders the declaration so ambiguous to be meaningless, as in, "We are not discussing any plans to attack *at this time.*" This statement can be interpreted as follows: (1) There are no plans to attack, (2) Plans to attack have already been discussed, (3) Plans to attack will be discussed at a later date, (4) There is no discussion about attacking at this exact moment. (Compare to Ambiguity)

Quid Pro Quo: The payback one receives for contributing to a successful political campaign. Campaign contributions pay off at least 100 to 1. They are the best form of investment possible. That is why one bets on both sides. Once the New American Century ushers in complete unicameralism—the one party system—payback for monies will go to the highest bidder in the case of conflicting interests. (See Pork)

Quota: Making a workforce look like the locals, minority-wise. Always assume that quotas smack of reverse discrimination—pushing aside the more qualified white guy in favor of political correctness—regardless of the abilities of the person chosen. That way, the flames of prejudice and divisiveness will always be stoked.

Quoting: The art of taking an opponent's words out of context to either embarrass the liberal bastard or to make it seem as if he agrees with your point of view. As well, one may quote an ally or notion by omitting anything that might be misconstrued or potentially damaging.

R is for RELIGION

Race Card, The: The Race Card is to be used whenever and wherever possible by putting a minority that supports the New American Century in a position of power, thus trumping the liberal opposition of being called bigoted for opposing such nominations.

Radar Screen, The: A euphemism for the people's attention. That which sails under their noses without detection has passed "under the Radar Screen." (See Diversion)

Rage: There's plenty of rage going on in America and that's a good thing because a population that's all whipped up about something hasn't got the time to get at the root cause of it all.

Rand, Ayn (1905–1982): "My philosophy, in essence, is the concept of man as a heroic being, with his own happiness as the moral purpose of his life, with productive achievement as his noblest activity, and reason as his only absolute." Founder of the philosophy of Objectivism and authoress of *Atlas Shrugged* and *The Fountainhead*, Ms. Rand remains a heroine and role model for the New American Century. In order to live up to her ideals it is up to every good American to create fantastic new machines or make incredible discoveries and withhold them from undeserving mankind, sharing only with people as worthy as oneself, i.e., a small group of super humans.

Rape Rooms: Torture chambers in Arabian countries, rec rooms in Afghanistan, backrooms at fraternity parties or hotel rooms at Tailhook reunions.

Rapprochement: Another sissified French word. Americans mend fences, bury the hatchet or bind old wounds. They don't go around kissing each other on the cheek.

RAWA: The Revolutionary Association of the Women of Afghanistan. Founded in 1977, these plucky Afghan femmes have battled misogyny and Soviet domination in their home country. Now that America has liberated Afghanistan and helped elect its new leader, Hamid Karzai, RAWA is becoming something of a nuisance with their yammering and name-calling. Just because they have backpedaled a bit as far as women's rights are concerned that doesn't mean our humanitarian venture into that country isn't a rousing success. In fact, we are doing such a good job that Mr. Karzai has begged us to stay on.

Reagan, Ronald W. (1911–2004): The Gipper, America's 40th President, the first Teflon President, hero of Grenada and first leader whose memorization skills were less than that of the average citizen. Ronald Reagan touched off the so-called Reagan Revolution by reversing the obnoxious trend of fiscal conservatism and environmental concern that so dominated the old Republican Party. His administration raised taxes, vastly increased the size of government and presided over America's first transition from a creditor nation to a debtor nation. His domestic contributions also include making ketchup a major food, union busting, facilitating the consolidation of media power and creating 17 million low paying jobs so that families could have two incomes, thus creating the latchkey kid society. Despite all the work done before and after his presidency, Reagan is remembered as having single handedly defeated the Soviet Union. More importantly, he is remembered for having honored the SS as German patriots at a cemetery in Bitberg, Germany, thus signaling the true beginnings of the New American Century. All in all, the greatest hero the world has ever known. Future generations will fondly recall how he chopped down the cherry tree, confounded the elders at the temple and freed the slaves. His wartime exploits are preserved in the pages of the Reader's Digest.

Recess Appointment: When the Senate fails to do its job and doesn't rubber stamp a Presidential appointee, all the President has to do is wait them out; for they cannot be in session forever. During their recess the President can then slip appointees in at his pleasure. Two of President Bush's latest are Alice Fisher, who is prosecuting Jack Abramoff (wink, wink) and, of course, John Bolton, temporarily our man in the UN.

Reconstruction: In the aftermath, clearing out the rubble and slapping on a coat of paint—regardless whether there are any civilians left in the neighborhood—constitutes rebuilding a school.

Reconstructionism: The reworking of government, education and just about everything so as to fit in with Biblical ways of getting it done. Apparently, Jesus can't get back into the game unless we, the people, set things up right for him. In a way, that seems to run a bit counter to the idea that while humans are incapable of their own redemption, it appears that they are quite capable of keeping the Lord from making a visit. Whatever. As long as Jesus doesn't interfere with the New American Century then it's all right to make preparations.

Recovery: The constant condition of the American economy. Since the wealth of the nation is distributed throughout the populace it is apparent that all of the wealth will never be entirely in the hands of those who deserve it and therefore, a never-ending recovery of the wealth by the rich is necessary.

Recruitment: Without a draft, it is necessary to do the hard sell to populate today's volunteer army. Thanks to education reform, outsourcing and free trade, getting recruits is not impossible. Also, there is the recruiting of foreigners with the promise of the fast track to citizenship. Be all that you can be, Pedro!

Recuse: To avoid a conflict of interest, one may recuse oneself from some group, operation, panel, etc. One should only recuse oneself if and only if one has better things to do. After all, if you have an interest in whatever is being examined, you ought to hang on as an expert in the matter and protect those interests.

Redact: The art of blanking out any information you want to hide from snoopers. You can only redact in the name of national security but who's going to know if you blank it out? The truth is, the ▓▓▓▓▓▓▓▓ has the power to redact any and all ▓▓▓▓▓▓▓▓▓▓▓▓▓▓ unless there is a ▓▓▓▓▓▓▓▓▓▓▓ Under FOIA, documents ▓▓▓▓▓▓ and ▓▓▓▓▓ but that is just a ▓▓▓▓▓▓▓▓.

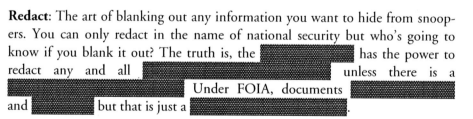

Redistricting: On occasion, particularly following a census, it is necessary to alter the representative districts due to population growth and shift. As a matter of course, these shifts will favor one party or the other because of the demographics of the area. Redistricting that favors the Republicans is a positive step toward creating the one party system necessary to the New American Century and obviously, redistricting that favors the Democrats is un-American, un-Godly and a terrible state of affairs.

Red States, The: The Heartland of America.

Red Tape: A euphemism for bureaucratic excess. In the insurance industry it is corporate efficiency.

Reed, Ralph: Former head of the Christian Coalition and heavy hitter for the New American Century in backing Bush, Christianity and the Warfare State. This cagey influence peddler harps against gambling while taking gambling money from Indian tribes via his buddies Ambramoff and Scanlon, one under indictment, and the other under close scrutiny for shady dealings.

Reform: Reform is a highly misused and misunderstood word. In no way does reform have to have anything to do with *improvement*. Taken literally, reform simply means to form again, to break down and rebuild in a different fashion. It is also an acronym for **R**emoving **E**very **F**orm **O**f **R**egulatory **M**andate. As a sop to the pharmaceutical industry: **R**epublicans **E**agerly **F**launt **O**vertly **R**uining **M**edicare.

Regulation: The diabolical enslavement of business. Regulation rips at the very fabric of free enterprise and freedom of choice. As corporations are model citizens of the New American Century it is incumbent upon government to keep its nose out of business. Business will regulate itself nobly, with dignity and restraint as it has always done.

Religion: There are many religions of the world and those that preach pacifism are false and devil inspired. Only religions that sanction preemptive war and have manipulative powers over their congregations have merit. To correct Marx, religion is *an* opiate of the masses—along with television, shopping, sports and, of course, opiates. (See Cult)

Religious Right, The: The spiritual warriors of the New American Century. The Religious Right will zealously commit to all military adventures and dictates of any Godly leader who seems to be hell bent on bringing Armageddon and the End Times to America. (See Useful Idiots)

Reparations: Repayments for actions taken by one's government that have done immense harm. Reparations are necessary and good when properly administered.

Reparations to General Motors for damage to their factories in Germany during WWII are an excellent example of reparations well applied. Reparations to African Americans for slavery and abduction are a bad idea.

Republic: That form of government wedged between democracy and oligarchy. America is a constitutional republic in name, advertised as a democracy, an oligarchy in reality.

Republican Party, The: The true keepers of the faith. All the other parties are so evil and monstrous that Republicans can do anything and still retain their loyal followers. There is simply nowhere else to go.

The Republican Party is synonymous with Conservatism despite the true definition of the term. No matter, as everyone else can be painted as kooky reactionaries or flaming liberals, the GOP is by default home to everyone scared to death of these types.

Retaliation: The rightful and proper act of swift and just retribution visited upon the heads of enemies of the New American Century for acts real or envisioned.

Retraction: When a factual error has been publicly disseminated it is incumbent upon the author to publicly correct the error unless it someway disparages the enemies of conservatism and/or the New American Century in which case it is excusable not to publish a retraction and to continue to circulate the rumor. If one does retract something, it should be published on an obscure page, in small print or if delivered orally, done in such a way as to reassert the original error.

Revelation, The Book of: The last and best book of the New Testament wherein Jesus returns as the settler of all old scores and the faithful witness of the glorious horrific end to most of mankind. Some believe that God's children will be taken up into Heaven during the Rapture so as to avoid the unpleasantness of the Great Tribulation. That would be nice but it may not come to pass depending upon whose interpretation you want to listen to. Either way, it'll be quite a change from the new normalcy.

Revisionist History: Commies and liberals are always trying to rewrite history so as to make Conservatives and Capitalists and all the positive things in life look bad and make themselves and their cohorts look good (if that's possible). Conservatives do not engage in Revisionist History. They rewrite history so as to correct any of the lies touted by those with a left leaning agenda, exposing the truth that liberalism has created all of the evils and ills of the world while right thinking people everywhere have always created unquestionable progress for mankind.

Revolving Door, The: The channel through which public servants become corporate heads and vice-versa. The welcome mat at the revolving door is always out.

Rhetoric: A fancy word for fancy talk. Rhetoric used to be one of the *four* R's—Readin', Ritin', Rithmetic and Rhetoric—but that last part of education was too thought provokin'. Rhetoric is the left hand of "watch what the left hand is doing while the right hand is picking your pocket" of American politics.

Rhodes, Randi: Yet another one of those insufferable Air America radio hosts. She is particularly annoying because she served in the Air Force and actually researches what she talks about. Thank God she's a woman. We can at least hold that against her.

Rice, Condoleezza: This child prodigy has wormed her way into the hearts of all good Americans. First she has a supertanker named after her then she becomes not only the first woman to be named Special Assistant to the President for National Security Affairs, but then goes on to be the Secretary of State. And a black woman at that! She's at least a twofer!

Condi (as she is affectionately called because it so whitens up her unspellable first name) may be well on her way to becoming the first woman President if she doesn't blow her creds like her predecessor, Colin Powell. She says she's not interested but then again, can you really trust what she says?

Right to Work: Wage slaves have a right to be free from union bondage and if any employer has the option between opening a "right to work" facility and a unionized facility it is his patriotic duty to opt for the former. Whole states are opting to be Right to Work states in order to get foreign corporations to outsource jobs to their precincts.

Ritter, Scott: This former Marine intelligence officer and the chief inspector looking for WMD's in Iraq has lost his marbles and keeps exposing everything the Bush Administration does. Not that it's a bad thing to anticipate another's moves but Ritter keeps informing the public and uncovering the actual motives and the underlying truth behind policies. As such, he is a danger to the New American Century and must be vilified.

Robertson, Pat (1930–): Another heavy hitter from the far religious right for the New American Century. Marion Gordon "Pat" Robertson, founder of the CBN (Christian Broadcasting Network) and the 700 Club is heavy into African diamond mines, gold mining interests with Liberian dictator Charles Taylor, mansions, the military and everything good about America. Pat ran unsuccessfully for President but wields a heavy political hand nonetheless. His recent faux pas concerning the assassination of Venezuelan Leader Hugo Chavez hasn't hurt him none: that was all blown away by Hurricane Katrina. But like a sufferer of Tourette's Syndrome, Pat had to pop off again—this time exclaiming that Ariel Sharon was laid low by none other than God Himself for giving away some of His real estate. Pat's getting a bit long in the tooth and we're getting a bit worried about him.

Rogue Nation: Any country that defies the IMF and the New American Century.

Roosevelt, Franklin Delano (1882–1945): The 32nd President of America and, of course, a Democrat because it was Roosevelt that brought in the hated New Deal. He will be remembered mostly as being a traitor to his class.

Rove, Karl: Bush's brain—the strategist behind many a GOP victory and chief formulator of dirty tricks, cover-ups and snares. This portly Senior Advisor blends into the woodwork and lets the pretty faces work his Machiavellian schemes but as they say, make no mistake about it, he's the architect behind the smear. In a candid moment, Rove admitted, "As people do better, they start voting like Republicans—unless they have too much education and vote Democratic, which proves there can be too much of a good thing."—thus reaffirming the need for No Child Left Behind.

Rumor Mongering: A perfectly acceptable way in which to deprecate one's enemies since if the rumor seems plausible it must be true.

Rudeness: Respecting others and having an open mind, being convivial toward others despite differences of opinion—these are the marks of a gentile and cordial society, certainly not the kind of behavior necessary in the New American Century. When people treat each other with kindness they tend also to cooperate in ways out of the control of their bosses and the government. America is about individualism, the rat race, competition amongst the lowly. Getting people to work together harmoniously is the business of the boy scouts, management or the military. When on their own time, the commons must be at each other's throats, suspicious and resentful of each other. Thus, cultivating a culture of open rudeness and haughty contempt is the order of the day.

Rumsfeld, Donald: Two term Secretary of Defense under GW Bush. "Rummy's" jaunty, devil-may-care attitude toward the war, the troops and homeland security has completely charmed the Washington Press Corps where he pontificates in Yogi Berra-like meanderings. For example, "I would not say that the future is necessarily less predictable than the past. I think the past was not predictable when it started."

Rumsfeld summed up the Bush Administration's attention to the needs of the military by stating, "As you know, you have to go to war with the Army you have, not the Army you want."

That may be true of a country that is under attack, but…Well, as long as you go in you might as well have a goal, as in finding the WMD's. Rummy gave the troops directions: "We know where they are. They're in the area around Tikrit and Baghdad and east, west, south and north somewhat."

Rummy also stated, "There are known knowns. These are things we know that we know.

There are known unknowns. That is to say, there are things we know we don't know. But, there are also unknown unknowns. These are things we don't know we don't know." It's no wonder he's a man after Dubya's heart.

S is for STATES RIGHTS

Sacrifice: No Sacrifice is too great to ensure the continued dominance, comfort and security of the upper classes. Of course, any Sacrifice necessary to meet these ends must be borne on the backs of underlings.

Sanctimonious: To act as if one were morally superior to others. Sanctimony works in the Heartland where one may melodramatically bemoan the plight of religious freedom, the elderly, children or any matter that tugs on the heartstrings without really having to do much about it.

Safety Net: The lowborn feel as if they deserve a "safety net" in order to rescue them from utter bankruptcy and poverty regardless of their indolence and foolishness. One has to be able to afford a net in order to have one. That is why the Safety Net is designed to help ailing corporations or executives from failure. Examples of features of the Safety Net are subsidies and the so-called Golden Parachute.

Satan: Beelzebub, the Prince of Darkness, Old Nick, Old Scratch, the Devil. The promulgator of all non-Conservative thought and action.

Saudi Arabia: Ah, the Saudis! Perhaps here is another example of the tail wagging the dog—or is it just cozy relationships between certain powerful influences in America and the world's largest oil exporter? Or is it perhaps that the Saudis are in something of an unassailable position, that being that Mecca and Medina are within their borders and as such nobody in their right mind would assault them? By extension, the Saudis get to claim that their whole country is *the* Holy Land, making it impossible for any other nation to do anything about their hijinks. Saudi Arabia gets a pass for all kinds of things that might get other countries into trouble. For example, they support terrorism in a big way and although America is fond of saying that in the war on terrorism, you're either with us or against us, apparently that doesn't include the Saudis. Even though the number one terrorist, Osama bin Laden is a native Saudi and is still well connected to the homeland, that seems to go under the radar screen. And even though 15 of the 19 hijackers on 9/11 were Saudis, that has not made a dent in our foreign policy. And even though the Saudi regime openly supports the destruction of Israel, we remain steadfast in our loyalty. The Saudis fund the *madrassas*, religious schools that foment hatred toward all non-Muslim people but that's OK. Who are we to get in the way of education? We have our "No Child Left Behind." They have their "No Child Left Untwisted."

Besides being such poor neighbors, the Saudis are poor hosts within their own borders. The government—the house of Saud—is about as repressive as any on earth. Their women are chattel and they cleave to a fundamental version of Islam that gives fundamentalism a bad name. Nevertheless, our leaders and the Saudi elite remain close friends and surely that will always secure the flow of ~~cheap~~ oil.

Saul of Tarsus: A.k.a St. Paul, the inventor of Christianity. Sure, Jesus had a few things to say but after Saul got zapped on the Damascus Road and turned from persecutor to proselytizer, he pretty much took over and wrote the guidelines. At first, the Christians were more than a little skeptical about Paul's conversion but Barnabas convinced them to be open-minded about it. In short order Paul began to dominate and steered things toward the way they are today. Perhaps one of the reasons he has such staying power was because he had so much staying power. Here was a guy who was shipwrecked more than once, jailed more than once, beaten, stoned, slapped around and finally martyred. His main claim to fame was that he always managed to keep it about things other than himself. A little humility goes a long way.

Scandal: Misdeeds by elected administrations in the New American Century are to be swiftly and justly dealt with. If done under a Republican administration, a scapegoat is to be quickly found and publicly chastised (unless the entire matter can be ignored, belittled and forgotten). For Democrats, every transgression must be made to cripple the leadership and denigrate the entire administration because Democrats live in the old American Century and have not yet wholly embraced the virtue and values of the new. For this they must be forever soundly rebuked.

School of the Americas: Established in 1946 in Panama then moved to Fort Benning, GA, the School of the Americas trained the military of many countries in the finer arts of warfare such as discrete intelligence gathering techniques and extralegal retentions and punishment. The School of Assassins, as it is fondly called, sported quite a graduate list including Panamanian dictator Manuel

Noriega, Bolivian General Banzer, Nicuraguan minister Somozas and Salvadoran death squad leader Roberto D'Aubuisson. If an atrocity is committed in any one of the Banana Republics, you can be sure it involves a few of the over 60,000 professionals trained in the past half century. Sadly, the SOA closed its doors in 2001 but it was quickly replaced by the Western Hemisphere Institute for Security Cooperation (WHISC). Rest assured that this new institute will carry on in the fine tradition of its predecessor.

Schultz, Ed "Big Eddie": A meat-eating, gun-toting lefty who is befouling the airwaves of America by disproving the notion that all progressives are namby-pamby, anti-2nd Amendment, sports hating creeps. Bid Eddie goes to-to-toe with the greats on respectable talk radio and as such is a threat to the New American Century! They've even got him a slot on the Armed Forces Radio Network poisoning the minds of our troops with his uncensored bias.

Schwarzenegger, Arnold: Austrian born "Governator" of California. Former world champion body builder, action hero and chairman of the President's Council on Physical Fitness, Arnold is currently attempting to get California in line with the rest of America by increasing deficits and cost of education to the poor while holding firm on tax breaks for the wealthy. Most of his time is spent hustling money from special interests in order to malign special interests. A man of the people, his engaging sophomoric attack style and funny accent have won him a place in the Heartland's heart. Sieg heil, Arnold. Gott mit Zie.

Science: Science is nice because it keeps America ahead of the technology curve but at the same time it can be a real nuisance when used to upset the apple cart. In the future, certain areas of science are to be downplayed. These include environmental sciences, evolution and stem cell research.

Science has for centuries been based on the use of the so-called scientific method wherein if something is repeatable under certain conditions then you can take that something to the bank. Well, that's just a theory and it's high time we called it such. Next time you fire up your car, remember it's just a theory that makes it work so don't count on it. That's also true of your light bulbs and just about everything else that's been manufactured on these theoretical bases. Now we all know that cars conk out and light bulbs fail so there have got to be holes in the theory somewhere. You can trust in God but you better take a closer look at science before you get hooked into believing in it.

Scruples: An archaic term for an idea that is outmoded in the New American Century.

SDI, The: The Strategic Defense Initiative, also known as Star Wars, is a proposed space and land based missile shield. In the hierarchy of national defense, SDI ranks as the technological high point. Said hierarchy is: SDI—Air Defense—Water (The two oceans)—Land Defense—FEMA—Local Defense—Duct tape and Plastic Sheeting.

If America can wrap herself in a defensive blanket then it will be possible to war anywhere else in the world without fear of having any property damage on our soil. That makes the idea of war so much more palatable, more acceptable, more chic!

Security: A nice fantasy. God made this world a dangerous, dangerous place and a Real American knows you really don't have any nor do you deserve any security. Nevertheless, just about everybody craves it. Therefore, the security business is booming and Patriot Act III is a-coming!

Self-Censorship: What the mainstream press does to itself for a couple of reasons—either it is afraid of reprisals by the government and/or upper management or it does so out of love for the people by not bothering their heads over niggling details that would only distress them.

Self-Esteem: It is un-American to have low self-esteem. Just being an American should fill one with enough self-inflating pride to last a lifetime.

Senate, The: That august body of legislators that is different from the House of Representatives in that it is not quite so representative. Since there are two Senators from every state that makes the smallest state (in population) as powerful as the largest. So it's kind of funny how it works out that there are currently 55 Republican Senators to the Democrats 44 (with 1 Independent) and yet the Democrats actually represent a slightly higher percentage of the population. No matter. That puts Republicans in the catbird seat and they are going to drive in the New American Century come hell or high water!

Separation of Church and State, The: Atheistic nonsense promoted by Satan and his earthly minions. Like the Bible, God wrote the Constitution through the hand of the Founding Fathers. Therefore, it is impossible to separate His church from America. Of course, there are any number of false churches and out and out wrong religions that need to keep their distance and that's perfectly OK. That's really Separation of Cults and State.

Seven Deadly Sins, The: Originally, they were Pride, Envy, Anger, Avarice, Gluttony, Lust and Sloth. Ok, sloth is bad but the rest of these are useful attributes! The *real* Seven Deadly Sins are competition, communism, land reform, progressive taxation, true democracy, unionism and regulation.

Seven Heavenly Virtues, The: These were Faith, Hope, Charity, Fortitude, Justice, Temperance and Prudence. The Seven Heavenly Virtues of the New American Century are Success, Power, Wealth, Strength, Nerve, Supremacy and Profit.

Seven Sisters, The: The original Seven Sisters were Exxon, Shell, BP, Gulf, Texaco, Mobil and Chevron Oil Companies.

Shadow Government, The: Churchill referred to it as the "Grand Cabal," a mysterious extra-governmental confederation of the super powerful rumored to be pulling the strings on the established authorities of the world. As all democracies on earth are really republics where a single spokesperson is elected to represent a larger group, it is useful to think of one's elected officials as liaisons to the Shadow Government in the same way one thinks of high priests, popes and mullahs as conduits to God. That way, one doesn't have to worry. So forget about it.

Shame: An impediment to any successful political career. One must be ready, willing and able to cast the first stone whenever politically expedient regardless if one is guilty of the same error. If caught in an embarrassing situation, it is always best to brazen it out although some-times (feel the political winds) it is good to shamelessly put on a display of shame in order to gain public sympathy. There's no shame in playing the repentance card!

Sharon, Ariel (1928–): Current Prime Minister of Israel. You have got to admire this man's chutzpah for going up to the Dome of the Rock to inflame the Muslims to start the current Intifada. Things have been a bit dicey under this stern PM and he seems to be charting his own course in a lot of ways, thumbing his nose at America on a number of occasions. But what are you going to do?

Recently, Sharon has been clearing Jews from settlements in a little bait and switch whereby new settlements can be started elsewhere out of the limelight.

Nevertheless, as Pat Robertson tells us, he has been laid low by a stroke from God for his perfidy.

Sheehan, Cindy: Being a youth minister who raised an eagle scout was simply not enough for this grieving mother. According to our beloved and ever-vigilant media watchdogs, we now know that she is merely capitalizing on her own son's death in order to gain some sort of public notoriety. And the rabid left is jumping onto the bandwagon. Her little stunt of camping out by the President's ranch caused quite a ruckus in Crawford but obviously failed to put a damper on GW's midyear break.

Sheeple: The vast majority of Americans. As long as the populace is content to graze through shopping malls and are secure that Big Brother is watching over the flock then they will happily be fleeced and sent to the slaughter.

Shock & Awe: Using careful planning, pinpoint accuracy, smart weaponry and incendiary devices to obliterate a target with such overwhelming force and ferocity that it delivers a knockout punch and demoralizes the enemy at the beginning of round one. To be followed by the Quagmire.

Shopping: The patriotic duty of all Americans (and all citizens of the world, for that matter). The poor in possessions are in their situation because they don't shop enough. Shopping gives one a true sense of accomplishment and satisfaction. It is one of the pillars of modern life.

Sinclair, Upton (1878–1968): Famous lefty author and would-be politician whose most famous work was *The Jungle*, an exposé on working conditions in the meat packing industry—now considered a wonderful blueprint for employment practices in the New American Century. Sinclair was once arrested for reading the 1st Amendment to a crowd of strikers.

Single Payer: A heinous scheme to funnel all of the moneys related to health insurance through one single source, thereby eliminating the need for the costly overhead of multiple bureaucracies and simplifying the rate structure of insurance companies. This scheme smacks of efficiency and governmental oversight and cannot be tolerated.

Skull & Bones: How extremely improbable is it that two members of a secret society in a hoity-toity university that allows for only fifteen or so new members a year happen to turn up as the only viable choices for an American election? It just goes to show you what a small world we live in.

Slam Dunk: People wrongly assumed that former CIA Director George Tenet said that finding WMD's in Iraq was a Slam Dunk. Actually, the Slam Dunk was about the *pitch* to sell the American people the prospects of finding WMD's in Iraq. He was pretty much right. The American people bit into that one hook, line and sinker until we didn't actually find any. No matter. Once the idea that we actually went into Iraq to liberate the Iraqis was dangled in front of them they lost interest in WMD's as fast as an attention deficit toddler on a cola and candy bar binge.

Slavery: Chattel slavery was a bit overdone and had to go as an American institution. Its replacements, wage and debt slavery suffice with so much more subtlety and covers a far broader slice of the populace. The next step is to link the fortunes of all the wage slaves to the Stock Market through Social Security reform thus making them slaves to the vagaries and machinations of Wall Street as well.

This is not to say that slavery has entirely disappeared from the shores of America. There is still a lucrative child prostitution industry that does quite well as long as we can keep producing children or importing them. Also, there is a small trade in incoming illegal immigrants that are sold as domestic servants, sweatshop workers or into prostitution. Ironically, whereas the Underground Railroad was a mechanism that secreted slaves from their masters into freedom, slavery in America has itself gone "underground." That is, of course, speaking of the 50 states. In American territories such as Saipan, slavery is quite overt but you can't prove that to Tom DeLay, who has spent plenty of time on the island but has yet to see anything unseemly.

Sleaze: Liberal campaign and political strategy. Conservatives reluctantly delve in negativity in order to expose their heinous opponents.

Slippery Slope, The: A metaphor for accepting laws and policies that will invariably lead to abuses. The slippery slope runs parallel to the Stairway to Success. That is, one may continually climb to ever more bountiful heights toward that ultimate American Dream but all it takes is one step leftward to be on the slippery slope to Godless communism, liberality and the destruction of America as we know it.

Smart Bombs: Weaponry capable of homing in on a specified target instead of gliding in on a wing and a prayer. Smart bombs are humanitarian bombs because they only kill the bad guys targeted. To be used in conjunction with cluster bombs in order to make sure.

Smart Border Agreement, The: As America moves to sew up its southern border using out of work xenophobes, the US and Canada have struck a border agreement to keep things safe for America on its northern side. Both countries are getting their identification act together—see National Identity Card—to keep track of the flow of people. One neat side effect—no more draft dodgers. Unlike in the Vietnam War, Canada will cooperate with America by not letting any draft age kids get into Canada to escape the coming empirical wars.

Sneak and Peek: Under the Patriot Act, law enforcement officials may obtain a so-called Sneak and Peek warrant wherein they get to break into someone's property while they're away, rifle through the place leaving it looking as if it were undisturbed. Thus, the property owner never knows he's been investigated. Pretty spiffy, eh? The best part is that the people who never suspect they've been "sneaked and peeked" are exactly the type of people who either believe they are immune from such treatment or simply don't believe the government would do that to *them*. People who naturally suspect the government already think they've been hit so it really doesn't matter—they're the type that always squawk so much that nobody listens.

Snowflakes: Snowflakes are thawed out embryos that made it to personhood by way of *in vitro* fertilization. There are some 40,000 frozen embryos in America awaiting a chance at being snowflakes. Either they're just going to sit there and wait or be thrown out. It's illegal to harvest them for stem cell research. Heaven forbid that!

Social Conscience: The wealthy love the poor. They particularly enjoy spreading their largess upon the less fortunate in the form of soup kitchens, homeless shelters and the like. The middle class, unlike the helpless and downtrodden can fend for itself as far as the necessities of life are concerned but they too are to be nourished in the form of patronage to museums and the arts. That way, they can be somewhat civilized.

Social Darwinism: Darwin's flawed biological theories applied to the social structure of mankind—that being "survival of the fittest"—an apt philosophy in the New American Century. Social Darwinism fits nicely into the Ownership Society, as he who owns the most is the most fit and he who owns the least stays that way. If you can't pay the freight stay out of the kitchen.

Ironically, the religious right believes in a sort of Social Darwinism despite their hatred for Darwinism. That is, they believe that the socially advanced, i.e., the wealthy and the powerful have been granted their station by the Grace of God. The poor, the downtrodden and the unhealthy of body (at least those who cannot afford the finest of doctors and health care) have been so situated by the Wrath of God. One can imagine this as a sort of divine spectrum, ranging from the extremes of the Lord's disdain to his highest esteem with varying degrees in the middle. Where the actual shift from scorn to favor occurs is up to conjecture but carrying the analogy to its natural conclusion must put this shift somewhere in that purple region between red and blue.

Social Security: Because Social Security has been one of the most successful, trustworthy and non-corrupted government programs it is an insult to Wall Street and an affront to the notion that government programs (with the exception of the military and corporate welfare) are useless, inefficient and crooked. Therefore, it is Communism of the first stripe. To give the great unwashed a sense of security in their old age is to relieve the burden of the old on the young and thus undermines a fundament of obligation that has stood since time immemorial. Social security is against family and family values! Forcing people to be frugal and wise is beyond any American principle, especially if it means keeping money out of the Market. Life is a gamble and America's seniors should have the right to retire in opulence or die trying.

Social Security Trust Fund: It doesn't exist. It's just a bunch of IOU's to the tune of $1.7 Trillion in a filing cabinet in Washington, D.C.

Socrates: Socrates taught Plato who taught Aristotle who taught Alexander. Not a bad run in world influencing. The good citizens of Athens killed Socrates for being annoying because he went around showing people how screwed up they were in their thinking. That just goes to show that people didn't want to hear it then any more than they want to hear it now.

Sound Bites: Americans are always diet conscious, particularly when it comes to ingesting information. Lengthy, in-depth explanations tend to lose an audience. That's why it is crucial to administer news, ideas, slogans, etc. in small doses—Sound Bites—so as not to overwhelm and confuse the intended message.

South Korea: The third Axis of Evil but also a little bit of the 800 pound gorilla in the room no one wants to notice because this is one country that can bite back. So we will try to use diplomacy even if it has to be with their little pygmy maniacal leader.

Sovereignty: *Sovereignty* means that you've got *sovereignty* over your country. Right now, Iraq may not have complete *sovereignty* but just as soon as they can take care of themselves we'll let them have it. Some countries just don't seem to ever get the hang of it. Take Haiti, for example. Every time they get *sovereignty* over themselves they go and mess it up to where we have to replace their elected leaders with people who know how we want things run down there.

Special Interests: Liberals love trial lawyers, nurses, teachers, unions and any other commie type organization that they can get money from. Then they go ahead and pander to these Special Interests at every turn. It's disgusting. Conservatives, on the other hand, only have interest in what is absolutely best for corporations and mankind. If one must say that they have "special" interests, they are in God, business, country, family and everything else that is good and wholesome.

Spin: The skillful rendering of news items so as to benefit the New American Century and deride its detractors. The first order of any media organization that spins the news is to profess to be even-handed and fair, thus putting a spin on its own credentials.

Spirituality: Not to be confused in any way, shape or form with Religion. Spirituality leads to inner awareness and universal consciousness. Those afflicted with a spiritual sense are a danger to consumerism, jingoism, mass manipulation and all of the virtues of American society.

States Rights: The government should not interfere with any state law with regards to deregulation, religious freedom and the like. Liberal laws are damaging to everyone and the federal government owes it to the state's citizens to step in and overrule.

Status Quo: Old Italian term referring to the way things run in life, the powers that be, "city hall", etc. While the multi-national corporations have got just about everything going their way, the Status Quo is still not quite good enough—they want absolutely everything to go their way and in the New American Century it will.

Stealth Candidate: Stealth is nac. It's like under the radar—sneaky. A Stealth Candidate is sneaky for Jesus. He or she comes on like a regular person but is really ready to pull out all the stops for the Lord. Comes in under the radar and wham! Pretty nac, huh?

Stop Loss: Enhanced enlistment—a bit like mandatory overtime for soldiers—wherein servicemen are allowed to keep themselves on the payroll after their hitch is completed without having to go through the bother of reenlisting.

Strauss, Leo (1899–1973): German born Jew who immigrated to the United States, not to escape Nazism but to promote its underlying philosophy to many a pliant student at the University of Chicago. Not surprisingly, many of the people in the Bush Administration studied under him. His philosophy is mainly one of deception; that is, to keep the inner workings of the state secret from the general populace. Elite rulers "in the know" would sternly administer the unruly mob using various techniques to keep it placated and docile, yet willing to go to war at the drop of a hat. In short, Strauss formulated the New American Century, its ideals, practices and methodology.

Struggle Against Global Extremism: This is the new sage way to talk about the War on Terror. Get it? **S**truggle **A**gainst **G**lobal **E**xtremism. Pretty sagacious—that means wise—changing the name because the War on Terror seems to be becoming more like the War to Recruit Terrorists and that just doesn't sound right. And besides, if anyone in uniform is killed then they're killed in a struggle, not a war. That means the services can hold out on benefits and such.

Superfund, The: An attack on one of the basic rights of corporations—the right to pollute the environment for profit. This misguided legislation proposes that polluters pay for cleaning up of their messes. Fortunately, public-spirited members of Congress have quietly taken the teeth out of the law and as it should be, the public will have to pay the freight.

Subliminable: You know, those sneaky kind of techniques that you see but you can't really see because they squirt by so fast. *Subliminable* techniques are head games, trying to make you think and believe in something. They're *subliminable*. That means like the way a submarine goes under water they go under your brain, which is like an ocean. That's the sub part—they're there but you can't see them.

Subsidy: Critics call subsidies "corporate welfare" when it involves government handouts to rich multi-nationals in order to keep their profits appropriately high. So what?

Supreme Court, The: Many thanks to Rush Limbaugh for warning us that the liberals worship the Supreme Court as a nine-headed god that must have at least five liberal heads. On July 1, one of the heads died but it will soon be resurrected as a God-fearing, clear thinking, rational Conservative head and that will swing the court in the favor of righteousness and slay the nine-headed beast god of the lefty atheists.

Suspicion: Suspicion is a healthy trait in any good citizen. If everyone would just keep a weather eye out on everyone else then nobody would be free to get out of line.

Sweatshops: A derogatory name for places of employment in the third world by the crying crybabies who don't like outsourcing. Sure, people get hot and sweaty when they do actual work—something a lot of liberals are afraid of—especially in the torrid zones where most of these fine factories and workshops are located.

Swift Boat Veterans for Truth: A band of loyal Americans who served in Vietnam and were on the same continent as John Kerry was during that conflict who didn't see him do any of the heroic deeds he claims and therefore dispute them.

SWORDS: Special Weapons Observation Reconnaissance Detection Systems—robot soldiers now in the making. Soon, America will send robots into battle in this, the second (flying weaponized drones are the first) generation of mechanized fighting systems. Ultimately, Star Wars will give us eyes in the sky that can scorch anything that they can see. Once these systems are in place there will be no more sniveling from un-American peaceniks about endangering our youth in battle! All we'll have to do is sit back and watch the monitors for anything that crawls out from under a rock and fry its brains out. And that includes you, un-American peacenik!

Sworn Testimony: Only Democrats, Independents or Baseball Players should be forced to submit to sworn testimony and to have their lies published for all to see. Conservatives never, ever lie or have anything to hide so their testimony need not be under oath or made public and should only be voluntary—in fact, it is not only rude and unpatriotic to ask, it's none of anybody's business! The same goes for oil executives.

Sympathy: Like Love, an emotion to be used sparingly and restricted to close family, pets, friends and members of one's own religious affiliation or class. The more sympathy you have for others is directly proportional to how liberal you are. So keep it close to the vest.

System, The: The underlying way in which the world works—not to be changed in any way. If the System is perceived as being flawed in any way then blame must be placed on a few sacrificial individuals, thereby diverting public concern. As well, such sacrifices are to be used as proof that the System actually works. (See Martha Stewart)

T is for THEOCRACY

Taliban: On again, off again friends. Ronald Reagan welcomed these plucky Afghan students (Taliban means student movement) to the White House and hailed them as freedom fighters and revolutionaries akin to our own founding fathers. We gave them a pack of stinger missiles to help them rid their country of the Red Menace. Once this was accomplished, we soon learned that this bunch were somewhat repressive Muslim fundamentalists. No matter, as late as the beginning of 2001 we were sending them foreign aid money. Alas, our friendship went to hell on Sept. 11 of that year due to the Taliban's close ties to Osama bin Laden and friends. We had to quickly unseat our old pals and put Hamid Karzai and his buddies in the Northern Alliance at the helm. Who or what is this Northern Alliance? It's a bunch of "warlords"—on again, off again friends of ours who are somewhat repressive and even more misogynist than the Taliban.

Talking Points: Mass media in the New American Century is a collaborative effort. In order for the public to receive proper information, news is distilled into a short list of so-called Talking Points that have relevance. Of utmost importance is how these particular items are to be analyzed and portrayed. Anything harmful to the New American Century is to be downplayed and/or presented in such a way as to be a plus. (See Spin)

Talk Radio: A way for Joe Six Pack to vent the feelings and agenda of the talk show host. Callers who have the effrontery to disagree with the host are to be humiliated, jeered at and summarily dismissed, later to be derided by callers who wish to ass kiss the host and secure more time on the line.

Tax Reform: Obviously, reforming taxes is the duty of every good lawmaker. Reforming taxes means to lift the burdens off the wealthy, to roll back the progressive tax structure and enable every poor or middle class American to pay his fair share in order to keep his head held high as a good participating member of American society. Having the rich pay an unduly enormous share alienates the low born whereas leveling the playing field of tax rates instills a marvelous sense of self worth. Hurrah to the reformers! Hurrah!

Teflon: The substance on no stick pots and pans. When applied to Presidents, it renders them immune to the consequences of their actions. Teflon is outdated—Presidents of the New American Century are to be of no substance at all and cannot be held accountable for anything they do by virtue of this fact.

Television: The most powerful self-insinuating tool ever conceived. Television has taken over American society in a way no invading army ever could. Television is today's after dinner narcotic. It raises our children, promotes consumerism, moves families from the front porch into the tv room, takes us to places we will never take the time to go and shows us things we will never take the time to do—all in twenty second shifting scenes and quick sound bites. It tells us what to think, what to buy and how to live. The boob tube. The ADDD (Attention Deficit Disorder Device).

Temperance: A Heavenly Virtue whenever you're out in the public.

Ten Commandments, The: In the New American Century the Ten Commandments are making a strong comeback as the basis of America's legal system. As only two of the Commandments pertain to actual law, it remains a task for the judiciary to interpret the remaining eight to fit the legal system. Commandments 1, 2 and 3 strictly pertain to God. In fusing church and state it is then natural to insert the word America into these commandments with a few minor adjustments. To whit:

1. America is number one. No one is to proclaim otherwise.

2. America's symbol is Her flag. No one may revere any other symbol, nor may anyone desecrate it.

3. You may not criticize America for Her policies, words or deeds.

4. Commandment 4 is immaterial and counterproductive as it pertains to a non-working day.

5. Do not dishonor your father and mother by being openly gay, liberal or poor.

6. Kill only in the service of America.

7. Men—don't cheat on your wives except in a spirit of youthful indiscretion.
    Wives—don't do it. The stoning option may be revived.

8. Do not steal from the wealthy or the powerful if you value your neck.

9. Don't lie about your neighbor—there are libel laws.
    ["Neighbor" is an ambiguous term left up to one's interpretation. One cer-
    tainly does not consider some trailer park denizen as one's neighbor, for
    example.]

10. Keep up with the Joneses. Buy everything they buy. Possess everything they
    possess.

Terrorist: Anyone fighting for a cause that American disapproves—like environmentalists and animal rights advocates. Terrorists are totally useful idiots since
their actions fuel the indignation of Americans and make them willing to give up
all kinds of rights and go to war anywhere in the world. (Contrast with Freedom
Fighter)

Texas Futile Care Law: Signed into legislation in 1999 by Governor GW Bush,
the so-called Texas Futile Care Law allows hospitals to override family wishes in
cases where extreme patient care is deemed futile—usually where the patient cannot pay the medical bill. Finally, the right to life is linked to the ability to pay for
it.

That's Different: No matter how similar is a case, proposition, finding, action,
thought, word or deed in the New American Century to that of anything perpetrated under a liberal regime, there must always be some variance as will make
any comparison moot. For example, no matter the circumstances surrounding
the invasion of Iraq, it is required that every American gets behind the President
and lends total support to the effort. When Clinton committed troops to the
Bosnia conflict, one was required to question all motives and operations and
howl to the rafters because that was different. When President Bush nominated
Alito for the Supreme Court he <u>had</u> to have an "up or down" vote—no ifs, ands
or buts! Harriet Miers did not deserve the same because that was different.

Theocracy: The integration of Church and State.

Theonomy: The subordination of State to Church. The right church, that is. (See also Dominionism and Reconstructionism)

Third World, The: Anyplace in the world that can be exploited without having to worry about laws and the environment. The back lot behind America's back yard. (See NIMBY)

Three Strikes: Throwing away the key on the repeat blue-collar criminal. Three strikes and you're out of commission for a long, long time. White Collar criminals—especially those well connected to the top—get to walk free. (See Pardons)

Time: Time is a funny thing. There really is only one time—the present moment. But thanks to the human mind, one can dwell upon an idealized past and an idealized future and not have to be in the reality of the present. This is the condition called normal consciousness—flights of fancy every*when* but now.

Tolerance: Ok, our good friends the Jews have a Tolerance Museum and that's all right. But tolerance in pretty much anything else means that you are soft on gay marriage, flag burning and all kinds of other things disgusting to good Americans. We don't need tolerance. We need people to shape up or ship out. Tolerance leads to acceptance and when that happens, there goes the culture.

Torquemada, Tomas de (1420–1498): Promoted to Grand Inquisitor of the infamous Spanish Inquisition, many a tale abounds about the cruelty of this pious man. Regardless of the truth of just how cruel and vile this period was we thank the Inquisitors for reminding us that if something happened once it can certainly happen again. Coincidentally, the Grand Inquisition concerned itself chiefly with Jews and Mohammedans.

Torture: The use of torture is woefully misunderstood. Its critics cite that those under torture will say anything to alleviate their plight and so, as a means of gaining intelligence it is faulty at best. No duh! Torturing suspected evildoers isn't to get anything out of them—it's to scare the hell out of everyone else (and also to have some good old fashioned fun). When the target population knows you will stop at nothing, they begin to volunteer information and squeal on each other in terror. Like the death penalty, what good does it really do to kill someone? You've already got them under lock and key—they're out of commission. But it serves as a warning to everybody that you won't hesitate to do it. Besides, killing and torturing people can be a real hoot.

Totalitarian: Like a Dictatorship, a Totalitarian form of government is way more desirable than a democracy where the mob gets to stick in its two cents. Totalitarian regimes get to push aside all opposition, set up education the way they like and pretty much have everything their way. Imagine the New American Century able to assert itself without any constraints! Any government farsighted enough to enact Totalitarianism would be the envy of the world.

> *"The great strength of the totalitarian state is that it forces those who fear it to imitate it."*
> —Adolf Hitler (1889–1945)

Total Recall: The exact opposite of "I don't remember", the three most important words in any Senate hearing or investigation of any kind. Detractors will scoff and think the worse of anyone who invokes his or her right to forget but this is a time-tested method for clamming up and has been used by the best of them.

Town Hall Meeting: A gathering of selected loyal individuals with pre-scripted questions asked in a pseudo-random manner of a member of the administration. Said gathering is to be in a cozy setting, evoking a completely genuine mood.

Trade Deficit: Thanks to outsourcing, lower wages and child labor goods are cheaper outside America. Therefore, Americans have to buy more from the outside than we sell. Smart Americans will simply invest in multinationals and foreign countries. Problem solved.

Trade Unions: A devil inspired effort by workers to join together and attempt to leverage power to get what is not rightfully theirs. Unions are the bane of existence to the ruling class. Fortunately, it is easy to convince a good portion of the working class to reject unionism by stimulating their fear response and pitting them against one another.

Traitor: The lowest form of pond scum known to man. A traitor is someone who turns his back on country or friends or whatever and goes to bat for the opposition. People who were once affiliated with bad causes—communists, liberals or other such low types—and are now Conservatives, however, are not traitors.

They are just folks who have seen the light. But those who had once advocated Conservatism and now go against the New American Century—surely they will rot in Hell for their treachery!

Transparency: In order for a society to be truly free its government has to be transparent—that is, its workings must be honest and open for all to see. Like *that's* ever going to happen! Not on the New American Century watch. You can take that to the your secret offshore bank and smoke it! Transparency is for other governments. They need to be open and easily scrutinized. Otherwise, Uncle Sam might think that something suspicious is going on.

Treaties: Diplomatic agreements between nations that are timed such that when they outgrow their usefulness they are to be considered not worth the paper they are written on.

Trickle Down Theory, The: The incontrovertible *fact* that if the wealthiest people and corporations prosper then some of that prosperity will "tickle down" to all levels of society because when the tide comes in all boats that actually float will rise with the tide. Since this is the most desirable hydro-economic theory ever devised, it is imperative that everybody gets behind the rich and powerful and promote their general welfare, pumping the bucks their way at every chance. Also known as Reaganomics, Supply Side or Voodoo Economics.

Trucking: America's rails and highways are the arteries that supply the nation its goods and services and the trucks are the red blood cells that ultimately deliver the end product. Although rail is more cost and energy efficient, trucking can deliver from spot to spot and therefore speeds up the cycle of delivery, in turn pushing the pace of consumption. Deregulation of this industry is necessary in the New American Century in order to increase profits (for the conglomerates), fight unionism, open our borders to our southern brothers, increase fuel consumption and as a reward to the truckers themselves, work toward allowing a 16 hour workday!

Trust: In God we Trust. Otherwise, we verify. Of course, in the New American Century you must trust your leadership explicitly and follow all of their strictures.

Truth: There is truth and there is truth. In a proper religious context (ours), everything is absolute and you can bank on it. The Truth shall set you free. In a political context, it's best to avoid the truth as much as possible. The truth is dangerous and the public really can't handle it. Then again, what really is "truth"? We're not talking some namby-pamby notion about truth being relative or any such nonsense. What we're asking is—if something is controversial or there is room enough for a good dispute—then is it possible to know the real truth? From a pragmatic standpoint, it seems as though truth goes to the party who has the power to proclaim it and make it stick.

Turnspeak: Turnspeak is a tactic in which one attacks an opponent, but claims to be the victim of the attack. Hitler utilized this scheme to justify his invasion of Czechoslovakia in 1939 by faulting the Czech people for trying to start a regional war by claiming their land as their own. All in all a good tactic; one that will surely come in handy in the New American Century.

Turn The Other Cheek: Misunderstood directive from our Lord. Indeed, to Turn the Other Cheek means to submit and not retaliate but this does not apply to Americans or any other free peoples. These verses were spoken to people living in occupied lands. Coupled with Christ's instruction to "render unto Caesar," the commandment is clear: conquered peoples are to bear under whatever is dealt to them. A superior power must mete out justice in the form of capital or corporal punishment wherever and whenever necessary in order to democratize and Christianize the lowly heathens. That many of them chafe under correct discipline is a mark of their heretical uncivilized ways, for as in another Scripture we are to "know them by their deeds" and those that attempt to fight back merely advertise their ignorance of Truth and demonstrate why it was necessary to conquer them in the first place in order to save them.

22ⁿᵈ Amendment, The: Now here's a law that has outlived its usefulness. It's high time America had some real continuity in government and what better way than to allow a wildly popular President as many terms as he wishes?

Two Party System, The: For two hundred years America has operated on the so-called two party system wherein two major political parties dominate. (There are several minority parties but they are inconsequential nuisances populated by the lunatic fringe.) The two parties tended to play off each other in a check-and-balance game that served two purposes: (1) to prevent a radical element from taking over the government, and (2) to give the impression to the voters that they had a wide range of choice. After all this time it has become apparent that having two parties merely creates "gridlock" and prevents government from moving in a swift fashion. In the New American Century, government must be allowed to make quick decisions and not be encumbered by debate and other such time-wasting procedures. Therefore, it is time to retire the two party system in favor of single party dominance whose platform is, of course, New American Century ideals.

U is for UNCLE SAM

UK, The: The United Kingdom, a.k.a. Great Britain, a.k.a.England. Before the Revolution we were simply colonies of England and now we've so turned the tide that England is our bitch! They had their crazy old King George III and now we've got ours, baby.

Uncle Sam: The personification of America. Like God, Uncle Sam is a kindly but stern old man with a beard able to smite anything He pleases. Also, looking at the tax code and the annual budget He, too, works in very mysterious ways.

Under Funding: Under funding particular legislation is a sweet way of conning the public into thinking that you are doing something good for them while you really aren't. (See No Child Left Behind)

Underground Shelter: An underground facility equipped with the necessities of life designed to house those members of society deemed most important for the continuity of the American way of life. In the event of a natural catastrophe, atomic war or the like, a select few will undergo the rigors of living underground until such a time as it is safe to emerge and reclaim *sovereignty*. Those on the surface and their offspring who survive must perforce pave the way for the appearance of their betters and submit to their rule.

Underground, The: An apt metaphor for the place where dissidents and all other nay-saying types crawl into and hide.

Unilateral: Going it alone. That's what Uncle Sam always has to do despite his entourage of sycophantic ineffectual camp followers—the coalition of the "willing"—whose only use is to deny that America is taking unilateral action.

Uniquely American: The ability to hold down three part time jobs so as not to burden one's employers with bothersome benefits payments. As the saying goes: Arbeit Macht Frei!

Unitary Executive Theory: Now there's a mouthful that simply means that the President can do whatever he wants.

United Nations, The: Good when they agree with us, bad when they disagree. But as a permanent member of the Security Council we can always trump this ineffectual organization.

UN Peacekeeping Troops: A controversial blending of US troops with foreigners under the "control" of the UN. Xenophobic Americans think that America is giving up control and sovereignty to a one-world government, the UN, but they don't understand that the one-world government is going to be US in the New American Century. Besides, with American veto power in the Security Council, troops will only be sent to where America wants them to be sent and usually with an overwhelming number of US troops at the fore.

UN Resolutions: When applied to enemies, reasons for America to dispute allegations of unilateralism. When applied to Israel, ignored.

UN Sanctions: When placing sanctions upon countries that America dislikes the UN suddenly becomes useful again.

Up or Down Vote: Every nominee for any office put forth by a Republican President deserves an **up** or down vote in the Senate because it is their duty only to advise and consent to such nominees, not hold them up through chicanery or arcane rules because of liberal partisan humbuggery. Naturally, any and all means to forestall Democrat nominees is in the best interest of the American people. And, of course, in the case of Harriet Miers it was necessary to pressure her to quit before she embarrassed the President for picking her in the first place.

Useful Idiot: Anyone who can be scammed into going to bat for something that is actually not in his or her own best interest. Often times, radicals who are a bit beyond the pale are actually underwritten by their enemies because they tend to embarrass their own and help in mobilizing the faithful against their cause.

V is for VICTORY

Vast Liberal Conspiracy: There is a Vast Liberal Conspiracy that is trying to roll back all the wonderful gains of the New American Century. You know the list—America hating groups that swamp our homeland and drown out the real TRUTH with their overwhelming liberal media, their filibustering commie Senators and worst of all, their activist judges that dominate all the courts in the land. Fortunately, for every one of them there are plenty of Conservatives to counter their nonsense.

Venezuela: One of those innumerable Latin America countries—except this one is a huge supplier of oil to America and it is in the grips of a monster, Hugo Chavez. This friend of Fidel Castro is an affront to the New World Order and everything it stands for. Somehow, the good people of Venezuela must be taught that they cannot keep electing such riff-raff.

Vengeance: Vengeance is the Lord's and Americans are proud to say that as a Christian nation we obey Him. As proof, look at the people we have recently warred upon, imprisoned and rendered extraordinarily to other countries. The whole world knows that these people are entirely innocent of the events of 9/11! Have we taken revenge upon Osama bin Laden and his minions? No. We are not a vengeful nation!

Veteran: Someone who has already served their usefulness.

Veteran's Administration: A costly drain on tax reform promulgated out of a sense of simpering loyalty to veterans. Today's ownership society will see to it that veterans take the lead by owning their civilian status and stop trying to sponge off America just because they were in the service and maybe things didn't go perfectly well for them health-wise.

Victim: We all know what victims are. We have the most compassion for victims of catastrophe since these things strike randomly at rich or poor. Flood, fire, car wreck, disease—they can happen to anybody. Victims of terrorism or violent crime are martyrs to the cause, for their deaths can be used to promote the security state. Innocents killed in war are not victims at all. They are collateral damage. And people who claim to be victims of police brutality or due to circumstance of birth are just great big crybabies who got what they deserved and should just get over it. Of course, that excludes victims of reverse discrimination where some worthless unqualified minority is picked over the superior white guy. That is a quota crime.

Christians and Republican public servants are victims of hate crimes by liberals who hate God and want to destroy America with their communistic ways. Everything they do (the noble Christians and virtuous Republican public servants) is vilified and a grand conspiracy to persecute them is always underfoot. They (the wonderful Christians and honorable Republican public servants) must therefore always be protected—laws and rules need to be changed in order to give them special fortification against Satan and his earthly allies.

Village: A liberal metaphor for their sick idea of extended family structures cooperating to raise a child into responsible adulthood. Everyone knows that all it takes to raise a child is a stern daddy with a razor strop and the gumption to use it frequently and a loving mom to apply mercurochrome to the welts.

Violence: America is a violent place. It grew out of violence and is keeping the tradition alive. We're a gun totin', in your face, rowdy sort of people and we're proud of it! That's what makes us and keeps us number one. Violence is tough love. You dole out a can of whoop-ass and the message is short and sweet.

Voting: A wonderful way to delude the populace into thinking that they matter and that their voice will be heard. Old Joe Stalin is said to have said, "Those who cast the votes decide nothing. Those who count the votes decide everything." How true. People already put their money and trust in electronic slot machines—paperless e-voting is just the next logical step!

W is for WAR

Wall Street: Home to America's financial district—where the big boys dope the ponies, so to speak, and the lowly take their chances.

War: That glorious enterprise that mends economic woes, cows the populace and whips them into a patriotic frenzy. War gives one peace of mind. It is first, foremost and always America's option and antidote to wasting time on diplomacy.

War Correspondent: Unlike the Ernie Pyle's of the past, today's New American War Correspondent sits in a hotel suite and relays news items given to him by a military liaison. Actual journalists who garner news outside of official channels are called targets.

Warlord: Any ingrate of a tribal leader who doesn't want to play ball with America. Warlords who do want to play ball with America are Freedom fighters.

Warmonger: A liberal term meant to negatively describe people who lust for and foment war. Now, one might suppose there are those in high command who seem a bit too eager for war but it serves a noble purpose in having them so loftily placed, for if a nation is perceived as being in the control of so-called warmongers then other nations will naturally defer to them out of practicality if not sheer terror. Warmongers thus displayed can then be said to act as deterrents in some cases. So, the loathsome peaceniks deride the very people who uphold the peace! Of course, if war should be inevitable, warmongers also serve an essential duty in being the first to hear the call without hesitation (with the exception of chicken hawk warmongers).

War on*: Insert Drugs, Crime, Poverty or anything one can convince the public to "war" on in place of *. These wars are, of course, really wars on the populace itself and are in no way intended to eradicate or even curtail the supposed intended objective. The true objective is to strengthen the security state, create new industries, new bureaucracies and make all sorts of things illegal in order to incarcerate more and more people.

As well, one can insert beloved things in place of * in order to convince the public that a plot exists to destroy traditions held close to their hearts. For example, it is widely said that there exists a War on Christmas by hoards of secularists bent on destroying Christianity itself. In truth, there are attempts to push back the overwhelming use of Christian iconography during the latter part of the year (now beginning before Thanksgiving) and the spread of Christian proselytizing in the public square. Each of these rebuffs are touted as direct assaults on the religion itself causing enflamed members to redouble their efforts to further attempt to Christianize every facet of American life. It's a win-win situation for the New American Century to keep the Christians and the secularists at each other's throats, playing them against each other in turn.

Washington Press Corps, The: Referring to a select group of reporters allowed to interview the President on rare occasions. In the New American Century, it is understood that no questions will be asked that might compromise our Fearless Leader or the Agenda. Admittance into the Washington Press Corps requires a thorough security screening and a long track record of professional journalistic experience—or not. (See Gannon, Jim)

Water: The property of American and multinational corporations worldwide.

Wealth: Many of the lowly aspire to riches. That is all well and good. Riches will allow you to buy a lot of goodies but you still have to play by the rules. Wealth—now that is truly the way to liberation, for wealth raises one above the common fray.

Wedge Issue: In order to keep from having to announce one's true agenda it is always expedient to create or resurrect a wedge issue, that being any irrelevant topic that enflames and divides the public. (See Diversion)

Welfare State, The: For a time, America was under the spell of Satan and his liberal agents. Together, they created the Welfare State that intended to steal some of the wealth rightly due to the military, corporate subsidies and foreign aid and spend it on the undeserving. The Welfare State is the exact antithesis to the ideals of the New American Century and the Ownership Society and thankfully, it has all but run its course. There are no free lunches—only free twelve course dinners.

Western Civilization: When asked what he thought about Western Civilization, Ghandi replied that it was a good idea and they ought to try it. That Ghandi had a mouth on him, didn't he!

Whining: Above all else whine. Remember, the squeaky wheel gets the grease. Win, lose or draw, whine loud and long. Complain how the liberals have got all the advantages, how they control everything and how they are not letting Conservatives have fair representation. A good example is in trade unions. Why aren't Conservatives running their fair share of trade unions? Why should labor unions continually back politicians who are for labor and not management? It's not fair! Get out and whine about it!

Whistleblower: No term can describe how despicable is a tattletale who rats on the secret workings of the New American Century. Whistleblowers in industry and the military are just as bad. Fortunately, since nobody likes a snitch it is usually possible to crucify the messenger and ignore the message. Take, for instance, the recent revelations concerning the President's circumvention of the FISA Laws and wiretapping without warrants. The government will certainly bring its full capabilities to bear—not in examining the legality of the warrantless searches but in finding out who was the traitorous leaker.

White Collar Crime: The perpetration of criminal acts against corporations or the business community at large. Crimes against the populace such as stock fraud are only considered criminal acts if they prove to be embarrassing to Wall Street. (Compare with Blue Collar Crime)

> *"Yea, death and prison we mete out to small offenders of the laws, while honor, wealth, and full respect on greater pirates we bestow. To steal a flower we call mean. To rob a field is chivalry; who kills the body he must die, who kills the spirit he goes free."*
>
> —Kahlil Gibran

White Man's Burden, The:

> Take up the White Man's burden—
> Send forth the best ye breed—
> Go bind your sons to exile

To serve your captives' need;
To wait in heavy harness,
On fluttered folk and wild—
Your new-caught, sullen peoples,
Half-devil and half-child.

Take up the White Man's burden—
In patience to abide,
To veil the threat of terror
And check the show of pride;
By open speech and simple,
An hundred times made plain
To seek another's profit,
And work another's gain.

Take up the White Man's burden—
The savage wars of peace—
Fill full the mouth of Famine
And bid the sickness cease;
And when your goal is nearest
The end for others sought,
Watch sloth and heathen Folly
Bring all your hopes to nought.

Take up the White Man's burden—
No tawdry rule of kings,
But toil of serf and sweeper—
The tale of common things.
The ports ye shall not enter,
The roads ye shall not tread,
Go mark them with your living,
And mark them with your dead.

Take up the White Man's burden—
And reap his old reward:

The blame of those ye better,
The hate of those ye guard—
The cry of hosts ye humour
(Ah, slowly!) toward the light:—
"Why brought he us from bondage,
Our loved Egyptian night?"

Take up the White Man's burden—
Ye dare not stoop to less—
Nor call too loud on Freedom
To cloke your weariness;
By all ye cry or whisper,
By all ye leave or do,
The silent, sullen peoples
Shall weigh your gods and you.

Take up the White Man's burden—
Have done with childish days—
The lightly proferred laurel,
The easy, ungrudged praise.
Comes now, to search your manhood
Through all the thankless years
Cold, edged with dear-bought wisdom,
The judgment of your peers!

—Rudyard Kipling c. 1899

Not a whole lot has changed in a century. As Ann Coulter puts it, "We should invade their countries, kill their leaders and convert them to Christianity." Alas, such is the task that God has given the white man to shoulder.

White Phosphorous: A.k.a. "Willy Pete." White Phosphorous puts up plenty of smoke, burns like hell, deep and hot. A marvelous weapon—not to be used on civilians while the cameras are rolling.

Whitewash: The art of painting a pretty picture over an ugly situation.

Windmills: Windmills that generate electric energy are an affront to everything we hold dear. They are a monstrous eyesore, dotting the landscape like silly little erector sets. A lovely *nucular* plant with a great impressive stack speaks of unlimited power, modernity and triumphant technology. Of course, the old massive creaky windmills of Holland are quite quaint and picturesque, not to be confused with anything practical that a good internal combustion engine could replace.

Winner Take All: The only way to run elections. Why should the majority give any scraps to the losers?

Winning: As the saying goes: it's not how you play the game, it's whether you win or lose. Winning is the only important thing in life. If (God forbid) one loses, one must do everything in one's power to make it seem like the other side cheated.

Wiretapping: Illegal wiretapping by the Executive is surely a crime so it is now up to Congress to make it legal retroactively!

Witch Hunt: What liberals go on when they perceive a misdeed by some fine, upstanding Conservative. The reverse is never the case. Law loving conservatives merely spare no expense, nor are they willing to leave any stone unturned in bringing the foul dealings of liberals unto the light of day. (Related to Inquisition)

WMD's: Weapons of mass destruction. Apparently, there were no WMD's in Iraq but since the ends justify the means and we are claiming that the ends are good, then it was all for the good that the specter of WMD's was a handy excuse to get rid of Saddam Hussein. (Truth be told, we invaded Iraq *because* there were no WMD's.) Nonetheless, we are always hopeful of finding a cache of something—anything!

Wolfowitz, Paul: The new President of the World Bank, former deputy secretary and undersecretary of defense and a founding member of PNAC, the Project for a New American Century. "Wolfy," speaking on foreigners meddling in Iraq following the American invasion said with typical Bush Administration irony, "I think all foreigners should stop interfering in the internal affairs of Iraq. Those who want to come and help are welcome. Those who come to interfere and destroy are not."

As a member of PNAC, Wolfowitz is truly one of the designers of the New American Century with its prophetic vision of a bright and shining future for all. "It's hard to conceive that it would take more forces to provide stability in post-Saddam Iraq than it would take to conduct the war itself," said Paul, demonstrating his soothsaying abilities.

Now Wolfy is the head of the World Bank, a position entrusted only to those individuals with impeccable credentials.

Women: Liberal women are overbearing feminist pie wagons that insinuate themselves into places and positions better left to real men because their wimpy leftist men folk can't keep them in line. Conservative women are strong, forthright, dedicated helpmates. Those that do rise to positions of power do so because of a higher calling, namely dispelling the vicious rumor that conservative men are misogynists.

WWJD: What would Jesus do? He would join the Republican Party, of course. What would Jesus drive? A Hummer. Where would Jesus dance? On the graves of homos, pinkos and anti-war protestors. At least, that's what a red-blooded All-American Jesus would do!

X is for XENOPHOBIA

Xenophobia: An unreasonable fear or hatred of foreigners—unless you're an American because all foreigners are a little suspect.

Y is for YAHOO

Yachts: A rising tide raises all yachts. While it raises all dinghies as well, since they are on a short tether, it raises them considerably less.

Yahoo: From *Gulliver's Travels*, Swift's (1667–1745) depiction of the Yahoo anticipated the average American by many a moon.

Yellow Cake: Saddam's favorite recipe, milled uranium oxide, known to chemists as U_3O_8. Despite the fact that he wasn't looking to buy any at the time the Bush Administration asserted that he was, it is still something that he could have been thinking of buying in the future and that made him a dangerous, dangerous rogue! What other chemical and biological agents was he contemplating? Thank God we headed him off at the pass.

Yin and Yang: The oriental pair of opposites signifying that everything comes equipped with its own shadow side and the two are inseparable, i.e., inscrutable oriental nonsense. Those things connected to the New American Century are wholly good, decent, honorable and wonderful and have no downside whatsoever attached to them. Liberalism is totally rank and there's nothing good about it at all!

Young Republicans: Storm troopers for God, country and the New American Century.

Youth: Tomorrow's cannon fodder, wage slaves or convicts. Yesterday's greatest generation. Today's sex objects. Youth must be monitored intensively (exempt Young Republicans).

Youthful Indiscretion: Any misdeed that occurred ten or more years in the past regardless of one's age at the time.

Z is for ZION

Zero Sum Game: In the game of life you've got your winners and you've got your losers. It all balances out in the end. Take war, for instance. One would think that war is a win-win situation with all its profits and political bonuses but if you take into account the grunts then it becomes a bit of a wash. That is, if you take the grunts into account.

Not every "game" is zero sum. There are lose-lose scenarios like *nucular* war and win-win scenarios like sunshine or clean rainwater but without a clear winner and a clear loser, the game just isn't worth the candle.

Zinn, Howard: Author of "A People's History of the United States" and other books that tell of a history that doesn't jibe with the one that everyone learned as a kid. His version of the past is not full of romanticized tales, myth and idealized legend. His heroes are not the Presidents, the Captains of Industry, Admirals, Generals and Baseball greats; rather, he dwells on martyred unionists, sweatshop workers, runaway slaves and underdogs of every stripe. He tells of massacred strikers and the hardships of Chinese railroad workers, of tenement fires, disease, bigotry and child labor instead of the uplifting stories of golden railroad spikes, tamed rivers and mighty ships of war. In short, Mr. Zinn's history is boring and un-American and should be forgotten. Only Children Left Behind will cleave to such nonsense.

Zion: Zion is symbolic of Jerusalem, of the Promised Land. In Christian terms, Zion also means the Promised Land for the Jews only because as it is foretold in the Book of Revelation, when the Jews get resettled the End Times can begin.

Zionism: Something of a misunderstood term. Zionism, in its simplest and most direct definition is "the movement to restore the Jewish people to a sovereign homeland of their own." (www.amfi.org/) Following this definition, who could be against that?

Zion, Protocols of: A fake document written in order to enflame the public against Jews in Czarist Russia. Supposedly, the Learned Elders of the Protocols of Zion intended through chicanery and masonry to take over the world. Despite it being exposed as a hoax, these fake documents are continually being rehashed in order to whip up a frenzy against the Jews. Keep a copy handy.

Appendix A

The New Declararation of Independence

Part 1—The Rough Draft

When in the Course of human events it becomes necessary for one people to dis-solve ~~the~~ political bands ~~which have connected them with another~~ and to assume among the powers of the earth, the ~~separate and equal~~ station to which ~~the Laws of Nature and of Nature's~~ God entitle[s] them, ~~a decent~~ respect ~~to~~ the opinions ~~of mankind requires that they should declare the causes~~ which impel them ~~to the separation~~

We hold these truths to be self-evident, that all men are created ~~equal~~, that they are endowed by ~~their~~ Creator with certain ~~unalienable~~ Rights, that among these are Life, ~~Liberty~~ and the pursuit of ~~Happiness~~. [Property]—That to secure these rights, Governments are instituted among Men, deriving their ~~just~~ powers from ~~the consent of the governed,—That whenever any Form of~~ Government ~~becomes destructive of these ends,~~ it is the Right of the People ~~to alter or to abolish it, and~~ to- ~~institut~~[h]e ~~new~~ Government, ~~laying its~~ [to] found~~ation on such principles and organizing~~ its powers in such form, as to ~~them shall seem~~ most likely ~~to~~ effect their Safety and Happiness. ~~Prudence,~~ indeed, ~~will dictate that Governments long established should not be changed for light and transient causes; and accord-ingly~~ all experience hath shewn that mankind are more disposed to suffer, while evils are sufferable than to right themselves by abolishing the forms to which they are accustomed. [Thus,] ~~But when~~ a long train of abuses and usurpations, ~~pursu-ing invariably the~~ same Object ~~evinces~~ a design to reduce them under absolute Despotism, ~~it~~ is their right, it is ~~their~~ duty, ~~to throw~~ off such Government, ~~and~~ to provide new Guards for their future security. ~~Such has been the patient suffer-ance of these Colonies;~~ and ~~such is now the necessity which~~ constrains them [and] to alter their former Systems of Government. The history of the present

~~King of Great Britain~~ is a history of repeated injuries ~~and usurpations, all having in direct object~~ [to] the establishment of an absolute Tyranny ~~over these States. To prove this,~~ let ~~Facts be submitted to~~ a candid world.

~~He has refuted his~~ Assent to Laws, ~~the most wholesome and~~ necessary for the public good.

~~He has~~ forbidden ~~his~~ Governors to pass Laws of immediate and pressing importance, unless ~~suspended in their operation till his Assent should be obtained; and when so suspended, he has~~ utterly ~~neglected to attend to them.~~

~~He has refused to pass other Laws~~ for the accommodation of ~~large districts of people, unless those people would relinquish the right of Representation in the Legislature, a right inestimable to them and formidable to~~ tyrants only.

~~He has~~ called together legislative bodies at places unusual, uncomfortable, and distant from the depository of their Public Records, for the sole purpose of fatiguing them into compliance ~~with his measures.~~

~~He has~~ dissolved Representative Houses repeatedly, ~~for~~ opposing with manly firmness ~~his invasions on~~ the rights of the people.

~~He has refused for a long time,~~ after such dissolutions, ~~to~~ cause others to be elected, ~~whereby the Legislative Powers, incapable of Annihilation, have returned to the People at large for their exercise; the~~ State ~~remaining~~ in the mean time exposed to all the dangers of invasion from without, and convulsions within.

~~He has~~ endeavoured ~~to prevent~~ the population of ~~these States; for that purpose obstructing the Laws for Naturalization of~~ Foreigners; ~~refusing to pass others to encourage~~ their migrations hither, and ~~raising the conditions of new Appropriations of Lands.~~

~~He has~~ obstructed ~~the Administration of Justice by refusing his Assent to Laws for establishing Judiciary Powers.~~

~~He has made Judges dependent on his Will alone for the tenure of their offices, and~~ the amount and payment of their salaries.

~~He has~~ erected a multitude of New Offices, and sent[d] ~~hither~~ swarms of Officers to harass ~~our~~ people ~~and eat out their substance.~~

~~He has kept among us,~~ in times of peace, Standing Armies ~~without the Consent of our legislatures.~~

~~He has affected to render the Military~~ independent of and superior to the Civil Power.

~~He has combined~~ with [the] ~~others to~~ subject ~~us to a jurisdiction foreign to our constitution, and unacknowledged by our laws; giving his Assent to their Acts~~ of ~~pretended Legislation:~~

~~For~~ quartering large bodies of armed troops among ~~us:~~

~~For protecting them, by a mock Trial from punishment for any Murders which they should commit on~~ the Inhabitants of the~~se~~ States:

~~For cutting off our Trade with all parts of the world:~~

For imposing ~~Taxes on us without our Consent:~~

~~For depriving us in many cases, of~~ the benefit of ~~Trial by Jury:~~

~~For transporting us beyond Seas to be tried for pretended offences:~~

~~For abolishing~~ the free System of ~~English~~ Laws ~~in a neighbouring Province,~~ establishing therein ~~an Arbitrary government, and enlarging its Boundaries so as to render it at once an example and fit instrument for introducing the same~~ absolute rule ~~into these Colonies~~

~~For taking away our Charters,~~ abolishing ~~our~~ most ~~valuable~~ Laws and altering fundamentally the Forms of ~~our~~ Governments:

~~For~~ suspend~~ing our own~~ Legislatures, and declar~~ing~~[e] them~~selves invested with~~ power to legislate ~~for us~~ in all cases whatsoever.

~~He has abdicated Government here, by declaring us out~~ of ~~his~~ Protect~~ion and waging War against us.~~

~~He has plundered our seas, ravaged our Coasts burnt our towns,~~ and destroyed the lives of ~~our~~ people.

~~He is at this time~~ transport~~ing~~ large Armies of foreign Mercenaries to compleat[e] the works of death, desolation, and tyranny, ~~already begun~~ with circumstances of Cruelty & Perfidy scarcely paralleled in the most barbarous ages, and totally ~~un~~worthy [of] the Head of a civilized nation.

~~He has~~ constrain~~ed our fellow~~ Citizens taken Captive ~~on the high Seas~~ to bear Arms ~~against their Country,~~ to become the executioners of their friends and Brethren, or to fall themselves ~~by their Hands.~~

~~He has~~ excite~~d~~ domestic insurrections ~~amongst us,~~ and ~~has~~ endeavou~~red~~ to bring on ~~the inhabitants of our frontiers, the merciless Indian Savages whose known rule of warfare, is~~ an undistinguished destruction of all ages, sexes and conditions.

~~In~~ every ~~stage of these Oppressions We have~~ Petitioned for Redress ~~in the most humble terms: Our repeated Petitions have~~ [is to] been answered only by repeated injury. A Prince, whose character is thus marked by every act which may define a Tyrant, is ~~unfit~~ to ~~be the~~ rule~~r of a free~~ people.

~~Nor have We been wanting in attentions to our British brethren. We have warned them from time to time of attempts~~ by ~~their legislature to extend an~~ unwarrantable jurisdiction over ~~us. We have reminded~~ them ~~of the circumstances of our emigration and settlement here. We have appealed to their native justice and magnanimity, and we have conjured them by the ties of our common kindred to disavow these usurpations, which would inevitably interrupt our connections and correspondence. They too have~~ been deaf to the voice of justice and ~~of consanguinity. We must, therefore, acquiesce in the necessity, which~~ denounces ~~our Separation, and hold them, as we hold~~ the rest of mankind, ~~Enemies in War, in Peace Friends.~~

~~We,~~ therefore, the Representatives of the United States of America, in General Congress, Assembled, appealing to the Supreme Judge of the world for the rectitude of our intentions, do, in the[y] Name, ~~and by Authority of the good People~~

~~of these Colonies,~~ solemnly publish and declare, That these United ~~Colonies are,~~ ~~and of Right ought to be Free and Independent~~ States, ~~that they~~ are Absolved from all Allegiance[s] ~~to the British Crown, and that all political connection~~ ~~between them and the State of Great Britain, is and ought to be totally dissolved;~~ and ~~that as Free and Independent States, they~~ have full Power to levy War, conclude Peace contract Alliances, establish Commerce, and to do all other Acts and Things which Independent States may of right do.—And for the support of this Declaration, with a firm reliance on the protection of Divine Providence, we mutually pledge to each other ~~our Lives, our Fortunes and~~ our sacred Honor.

Part 2—The Final Draft

The New Declaration of Independence of the *nited States of America*

When in the Course of human events it becomes necessary for one people to dissolve political bands and to assume among the power of the earth the station to which God entitles them, respect the opinions which impel them.

We hold these truths to be self-evident that all men are created, that they are endowed by the Creator with certain Rights, that among these are Life and the pursuit of Property—that to secure these rights, Governments are instituted among Men, deriving their powers from God. It is the Right of the People in the Government to found its powers in such form as to most likely effect their Safety and Happiness. Indeed, all experience hath shewn that mankind are more disposed to suffer, while evils are sufferable than to right themselves by abolishing the forms to which they are accustomed. Thus, a long train of abuses and usurpations so as to reduce them under absolute Despotism is their right. It is the duty of such Government to provide new Guards for their future security and constrain them and to alter their former Systems of Government.

The history of the present is a history of repeated injuries to the establishment of an absolute Tyranny. Let a candid world Assent to Laws necessary for the public good.: Forbid Governors to pass Laws of immediate and pressing importance unless for the accommodation of tyrants only:

Call together legislative bodies at places unusual, uncomfortable and distant from the depository of their Public Records for the sole purpose of fatiguing them into compliance.

Dissolve Representative Houses repeatedly, opposing with manly firmness the rights of the people. After such dissolutions cause others to be elected by the State. In the mean time, expose to all the dangers of invasion from without and convulsions within:

Endeavor the population of Foreigners their migrations hither and obstruct the amount and payment of their salaries:

Erect a multitude of New Offices and send swarms of Officers to harass people in times of peace. Standing Armies, independent of and superior to the Civil Power, with the object of quartering large bodies of armed troops among the Inhabitants of the States for imposing the benefit of the free System of Laws, establishing therein absolute rule:

Abolish most Laws and alter fundamentally the Forms of Governments:

Suspend Legislatures and declare the power to legislate in all cases whatsoever to protect and destroy the lives of people:

Transport large Armies of foreign Mercenaries to complete the works of death, desolation and tyranny with circumstances of Cruelty & Perfidy scarcely paralleled in the most barbarous ages, and totally worthy of the Head of a civilized nation:

Constrain Citizens taken Captive to bear Arms, to become the executioners of their friends and Brethren, or to fall themselves:

Excite domestic insurrections and endeavor to bring on an undistinguished destruction of all ages, sexes and conditions:

Every Petition for Redress is to be answered only by repeated injury. A Prince, whose character is thus marked by every act which may define a Tyrant is to rule people by unwarrantable jurisdiction over them. Be deaf to the voice of justice and denounce the rest of mankind.

Therefore, the Representatives of the United States of America, in General Congress, Assembled, appealing to the Supreme Judge of the world for the rectitude of our intentions, do, in thy Name, solemnly publish and declare, That these United States are Absolved from all Allegiances and have full Power to levy War, conclude Peace contract Alliances, establish Commerce, and to do all other Acts and Things which Independent States may of right do.—And for the support of this Declaration, with a firm reliance on the protection of Divine Providence, we mutually pledge to each other our sacred Honor.

APPENDIX B

The Bill of Rights as Interpreted in the New American Century

Amendment I

Congress shall make no law respecting an establishment of religion, or prohibiting the free exercise thereof; or abridging the freedom of speech, or of the press; or the right of the people peaceably to assemble, and to petition the Government for a redress of grievances.

(Christianity was well established in America even before the Constitution was ever thought of. Therefore, Christianity can be considered the religion of the land. As for speech—anybody can say anything they like. Certain things will get you in trouble for saying them—but you can say anything you like. "Or of the press"…that doesn't even make any sense. Anybody assembling for things that are looked favorable upon by proponents of the New American Century can assemble all they want. Nay-sayers, liberal hate groups and opponents by definition assemble in a non-peaceful manner because good citizens are going to have to clobber them. Therefore, it's best they don't get together at all. And as for the last thing—you can grieve all you want—that doesn't mean anyone is going to listen.)

Amendment II

A well regulated Militia being necessary to the security of a free State, the right of the people to keep and bear Arms shall not be infringed.

(For now, anybody that owns a gun is part of the militia of America. If it becomes necessary to round up the guns in order to protect the leaders of the New American Century then all bets are off and the only well regulated militia will be the police, the armed forces and the security state.)

Amendment III

No Soldier shall, in time of peace be quartered in any house, without the consent of the Owner, nor in time of war, but in a manner to be prescribed by law.

(We are in a continued War on Terror. So, whatever is necessary is prescribed by law.)

Amendment IV

The right of the people to be secure in their persons, houses, papers, and effects, against unreasonable searches and seizures, shall not be violated, and no Warrants shall issue, but upon probable cause, supported by Oath or affirmation, and particularly describing the place to be searched, and the persons or things to be seized.

(What's so unreasonable about Uncle Sam/Big Brother knowing what's going on in his own domain? Let's just say we need to know about bad guys, wherever and whenever—and whoever.)

Amendment V

No person shall be held to answer for a capital, or otherwise infamous crime, unless on a presentment or indictment of a Grand Jury, except in cases arising in the land or naval forces, or in the Militia, when in actual service in time of War or public danger; nor shall any person be subject for the same offence to be twice put in jeopardy of life or limb; nor shall be compelled in any criminal case to be a witness against himself, nor be deprived of life, liberty, or property, without due process of law; nor shall private property be taken for public use, without just compensation.

(We are in a time of public danger and in a continued War on Terror as stipulated beforehand. As everyone in America is in actual service of something then they fall under those cases mentioned as exceptions—everyone suspected of committing a crime is an enemy combatant. That is due process in the New American Century.)

Amendment VI

In all criminal prosecutions, the accused shall enjoy the right to a speedy and public trial, by an impartial jury of the State and district wherein the crime shall have been committed, which district shall have been previously ascertained by law, and to be informed of the nature and cause of the accusation; to be confronted with the witnesses against him; to have compulsory process for obtaining witnesses in his favor, and to have the Assistance of Counsel for his defense.

(Fine. Let the courts do their thing—only in the New American Century, said courts will surely be packed with true patriotic judges who know what's expected of them.)

Amendment VII

In suits at common law, where the value in controversy shall exceed twenty dollars, the right of trial by jury shall be preserved, and no fact tried by a jury, shall be otherwise reexamined in any Court of the United States, than according to the rules of the common law.

(Torte reform shall take care of this.)

Amendment VIII

Excessive bail shall not be required, nor excessive fines imposed, nor cruel and unusual punishments inflicted.

("Excessive", "cruel" and "unusual" shall be defined by the Attorney General.)

Amendment IX

The enumeration in the Constitution, of certain rights, shall not be construed to deny or disparage others retained by the people.

(This does not mean that there is a right to privacy!)

Amendment X

The powers not delegated to the United States by the Constitution, nor prohibited by it to the States, are reserved to the States respectively, or to the people.

(A useless appendage, since in the New American Century the government reserves all rights unto itself and will dole them out as deemed necessary.)

APPENDIX C

Signatories of the Statement of Principles Offered to the World by the Project for a New American Century

(www.newamericancentury.org/lettersstatements.htm)

Elliot Abrams—Deputy National Security Adviser, indicted during the Iran-Contra scandal of the Reagan Administration

Gary Bauer—Spokesman for the religious right

William J. Bennett—former Secretary of Education with numerous connections to right wing advisory groups and think tanks

Jeb Bush—Governor of Florida

Dick Cheney—Vice President of the United States

Eliot A. Cohen—Robert E. Osgood Professor of Strategic Studies at the Paul H. Nitze School of Advanced International Studies, Johns Hopkins University, military historian, commentator on current events and a self-proclaimed hawk

Midge Decter—Editor and founding member of PNAC, board of trustees of the Heritage Foundation

Paula Dobriansky—Under Secretary of State for Global Affairs, Vice President and Director of the Washington Office of the Council on Foreign Relations

Steve Forbes—Former presidential candidate and flat tax advocate

Aaron Friedberg—Vice President Cheney's Deputy National Security Adviser, Professor of Politics and International Affairs (Harvard), NSC and CIA Consultant

Francis Fukuyama—Bernard L. Schwartz Professor of International Political Economy at the School of Advanced International Studies, Johns Hopkins University, globalist and proponent of nation building

Frank Gaffney—Former Reagan administration Assistant Secretary of Defense, President and Founder of the Center for Security Policy and columnist for The Washington Times (founded by Sun Myung Moon)

Fred C. Ikle—former Under Secretary of Defense for Policy with many right wing institutional connections

Donald Kagan—Professor of History and Classis, Yale University

Zalmay Khalilzad—Current Ambassador to Afghanistan (2003), Unocal advisor, for Senior Political Scientist at the Rand Corporation

I. Lewis Libby—"Scooter", Chief of Staff to the Vice President, served under GHW Bush

Norman Podhoretz—Member of the Council on Foreign Relations, Senior Fellow at the Hudson Institute, Co-founder of the Committee on the Present Danger and the Committee for the Free World

Dan Quayle—former Vice President under GWH Bush

Peter W. Rodman—assistant secretary of defense for international security, also served in a number of Republican administrations, senior editor for the National Review (1991-1999)

Stephen P. Rosen—Professor of National Security and Military Affairs at Harvard University, defense stratgist

Henry S. Rowen—former Assistant Secretary of Defense under Reagan, member of the Council on Foreign Relations, Professor at the Stanford University Graduate School of Business

Donald Rumsfeld—Current Secretary of Defense

Vin Weber—former Republican Congressman (Minn.), lobbyist

George Weigel—Senior Fellow at the Ethics and Public Policy Center, Catholic theologian

Paul Wolfowitz—Current President of the World Bank

Conspicuously missing from this list are **William Kristol** and **Robert Kagan**, the founders of PNAC.

APPENDIX D

Eisenhower's Farewell Address to the Nation

1/17/61

Good evening, my fellow Americans.

First, I should like to express my gratitude to the radio and television networks for the opportunities they have given me over the years to bring reports and messages to our nation. My special thanks go to them for the opportunity of addressing you this evening.

Three days from now, after half century in the service of our country, I shall lay down the responsibilities of office as, in traditional and solemn ceremony, the authority of the Presidency is vested in my successor. This evening, I come to you with a message of leave-taking and farewell, and to share a few final thoughts with you, my countrymen.

Like every other—Like every other citizen, I wish the new President, and all who will labor with him, Godspeed. I pray that the coming years will be blessed with peace and prosperity for all.

Our people expect their President and the Congress to find essential agreement on issues of great moment, the wise resolution of which will better shape the future of the nation. My own relations with the Congress, which began on a remote and tenuous basis when, long ago, a member of the Senate appointed me to West Point, have since ranged to the intimate during the war and immediate post-war period, and finally to the mutually interdependent during these past eight years. In this final relationship, the Congress and the Administration have, on most vital issues, cooperated well; to serve the nation good, rather than mere partisanship, and so have assured that the business of the nation should go forward. So, my official relationship with the Congress ends in a feeling—on my part—of gratitude that we have been able to do so much together.

We now stand ten years past the midpoint of a century that has witnessed four major wars among great nations. Three of these involved our own country. Despite these holocausts, America is today the strongest, the most influential, and most productive nation in the world. Understandably proud of this pre-eminence, we yet realize that America's leadership and prestige depend, not merely upon our unmatched material progress, riches, and military strength, but on how we use our power in the interests of world peace and human betterment.

Throughout America's adventure in free government, our basic purposes have been to keep the peace, to foster progress in human achievement, and to enhance liberty, dignity, and integrity among peoples and among nations. To strive for less would be unworthy of a free and religious people. Any failure traceable to arrogance, or our lack of comprehension, or readiness to sacrifice would inflict upon us grievous hurt, both at home and abroad.

Progress toward these noble goals is persistently threatened by the conflict now engulfing the world. It commands our whole attention, absorbs our very beings. We face a hostile ideology global in scope, atheistic in character, ruthless in purpose, and insidious [insidious] in method. Unhappily, the danger it poses promises to be of indefinite duration. To meet it successfully, there is called for, not so much the emotional and transitory sacrifices of crisis, but rather those which enable us to carry forward steadily, surely, and without complaint the burdens of a prolonged and complex struggle with liberty the stake. Only thus shall we remain, despite every provocation, on our charted course toward permanent peace and human betterment.

Crises there will continue to be. In meeting them, whether foreign or domestic, great or small, there is a recurring temptation to feel that some spectacular and costly action could become the miraculous solution to all current difficulties. A huge increase in newer elements of our defenses; development of unrealistic programs to cure every ill in agriculture; a dramatic expansion in basic and applied research—these and many other possibilities, each possibly promising in itself, may be suggested as the only way to the road we wish to travel.

But each proposal must be weighed in the light of a broader consideration: the need to maintain balance in and among national programs, balance between the private and the public economy, balance between the cost and hoped for advantages, balance between the clearly necessary and the comfortably desirable, balance between our essential requirements as a nation and the duties imposed by the nation upon the individual, balance between actions of the moment and the national welfare of the future. Good judgment seeks balance and progress. Lack of it eventually finds imbalance and frustration. The record of many decades stands as proof that our people and their Government have, in the main, understood these truths and have responded to them well, in the face of threat and stress.

But threats, new in kind or degree, constantly arise. Of these, I mention two only.

A vital element in keeping the peace is our military establishment. Our arms must be mighty, ready for instant action, so that no potential aggressor may be tempted to risk his own destruction. Our military organization today bears little relation to that known of any of my predecessors in peacetime, or, indeed, by the fighting men of World War II or Korea.

Until the latest of our world conflicts, the United States had no armaments industry. American makers of plowshares could, with time and as required, make swords as well. But we can no longer risk emergency improvisation of national defense. We have been compelled to create a permanent armaments industry of vast proportions. Added to this, three and a half million men and women are directly engaged in the defense establishment. We annually spend on military security alone more than the net income of all United States corporations.

Now this conjunction of an immense military establishment and a large arms industry is new in the American experience. The total influence—economic, political, even spiritual—is felt in every city, every Statehouse, every office of the Federal government. We recognize the imperative need for this development. Yet, we must not fail to comprehend its grave implications. Our toil, resources, and livelihood are all involved. So is the very structure of our society.

In the councils of government, we must guard against the acquisition of unwarranted influence, whether sought or unsought, by the military-industrial complex. The potential for the disastrous rise of misplaced power exists and will persist. We must never let the weight of this combination endanger our liberties or democratic processes. We should take nothing for granted. Only an alert and knowledgeable citizenry can compel the proper meshing of the huge industrial and military machinery of defense with our peaceful methods and goals, so that security and liberty may prosper together.

Akin to, and largely responsible for the sweeping changes in our industrial-military posture, has been the technological revolution during recent decades. In this revolution, research has become central; it also becomes more formalized, complex, and costly. A steadily increasing share is conducted for, by, or at the direction of, the Federal government.

Today, the solitary inventor, tinkering in his shop, has been overshadowed by task forces of scientists in laboratories and testing fields. In the same fashion, the free university, historically the fountainhead of free ideas and scientific discovery, has experienced a revolution in the conduct of research. Partly because of the huge costs involved, a government contract becomes virtually a substitute for intellectual curiosity. For every old blackboard there are now hundreds of new electronic computers. The prospect of domination of the nation's scholars by Federal employment, project allocations, and the power of money is ever present—and is gravely to be regarded.

Yet, in holding scientific research and discovery in respect, as we should, we must also be alert to the equal and opposite danger that public policy could itself become the captive of a scientific-technological elite.

It is the task of statesmanship to mold, to balance, and to integrate these and other forces, new and old, within the principles of our democratic system—ever aiming toward the supreme goals of our free society.

Another factor in maintaining balance involves the element of time. As we peer into society's future, we—you and I, and our government—must avoid the impulse to live only for today, plundering for our own ease and convenience the precious resources of tomorrow. We cannot mortgage the material assets of our grandchildren without risking the loss also of their political and spiritual heritage. We want democracy to survive for all generations to come, not to become the insolvent phantom of tomorrow.

During the long lane of the history yet to be written, America knows that this world of ours, ever growing smaller, must avoid becoming a community of dreadful fear and hate, and be, instead, a proud confederation of mutual trust and respect. Such a confederation must be one of equals. The weakest must come to the conference table with the same confidence, as do we, protected as we are by our moral, economic, and military strength. That table, though scarred by many fast frustrations—past frustrations, cannot be abandoned for the certain agony of disarmament—of the battlefield.

Disarmament, with mutual honor and confidence, is a continuing imperative. Together we must learn how to compose differences, not with arms, but with intellect and decent purpose. Because this need is so sharp and apparent, I confess that I lay down my official responsibilities in this field with a definite sense of disappointment. As one who has witnessed the horror and the lingering sadness of war, as one who knows that another war could utterly destroy this civilization which has been so slowly and painfully built over thousands of years, I wish I could say tonight that a lasting peace is in sight.

Happily, I can say that war has been avoided. Steady progress toward our ultimate goal has been made. But so much remains to be done. As a private citizen, I shall never cease to do what little I can to help the world advance along that road.

So, in this, my last good night to you as your President, I thank you for the many opportunities you have given me for public service in war and in peace. I trust in that—in that—in that service you find some things worthy. As for the rest of it, I know you will find ways to improve performance in the future.

You and I, my fellow citizens, need to be strong in our faith that all nations, under God, will reach the goal of peace with justice. May we be ever unswerving in devotion to principle, confidant but humble with power, diligent in pursuit of the Nations' great goals.

To all the peoples of the world, I once more give expression to America's prayerful and continuing aspiration: We pray that peoples of all faiths, all races, all nations, may have their great human needs satisfied; that those now denied opportunity shall come to enjoy it to the full; that all who yearn for freedom may experience its few spiritual blessings. Those who have freedom will understand, also, its heavy responsibility; that all who are insensitive to the needs of others will learn charity; and that the sources—scourges of poverty, disease, and ignorance will be made [to] disappear from the earth; and that in the goodness of time, all peoples will come to live together in a peace guaranteed by the binding force of mutual respect and love.

Now, on Friday noon, I am to become a private citizen. I am proud to do so. I look forward to it.

Thank you, and good night.

APPENDIX E

Articles of Impeachment of Richard Nixon Adopted by the Committee on the Judiciary

7/27/74

Article 1

RESOLVED, That Richard M. Nixon, President of the United States, is impeached for high crimes and misdemeanours, and that the following articles of impeachment to be exhibited to the Senate:

ARTICLES OF IMPEACHMENT EXHIBITED BY THE HOUSE OF REP-RESENTATIVES OF THE UNITED STATES OF AMERICA IN THE NAME OF ITSELF AND OF ALL OF THE PEOPLE OF THE UNITED STATES OF AMERICA, AGAINST RICHARD M. NIXON, PRESIDENT OF THE UNITED STATES OF AMERICA, IN MAINTENANCE AND SUPPORT OF ITS IMPEACHMENT AGAINST HIM FOR HIGH CRIMES AND MISDEMEANOURS.

ARTICLE 1

In his conduct of the office of President of the United States, Richard M. Nixon, in violation of his constitutional oath faithfully to execute the office of President of the United States and, to the best of his ability, preserve, protect, and defend the Constitution of the United States, and in violation of his constitutional duty to take care that the laws be faithfully executed, has prevented, obstructed, and impeded the administration of justice, in that:

On June 17, 1972, and prior thereto, agents of the Committee for the Re-election of the President committed unlawful entry of the headquarters of the Democratic National Committee in Washington, District of Columbia, for the purpose of securing political intelligence. Subsequent thereto, Richard M. Nixon, using the powers of his high office, engaged personally and through his close subordinates and agents, in a course of conduct or plan designed to delay, impede, and obstruct the investigation of such illegal entry; to cover up, conceal and protect those responsible; and to conceal the existence and scope of other unlawful covert activities.

The means used to implement this course of conduct or plan included one or more of the following:

1. making false or misleading statements to lawfully authorized investigative officers and employees of the United States;

2. withholding relevant and material evidence or information from lawfully authorized investigative officers and employees of the United States;

3. approving, condoning, acquiescing in, and counseling witnesses with respect to the giving of false or misleading statements to lawfully authorized investigative officers and employees of the United States and false or misleading testimony in duly instituted judicial and congressional proceedings;

4. interfering or endeavouring to interfere with the conduct of investigations by the Department of Justice of the United States, the Federal Bureau of Investigation, the office of Watergate Special Prosecution Force, and Congressional Committees;

5. approving, condoning, and acquiescing in, the surreptitious payment of substantial sums of money for the purpose of obtaining the silence or influencing the testimony of witnesses, potential witnesses or individuals who participated in such unlawful entry and other illegal activities;

6. endeavouring to misuse the Central Intelligence Agency, an agency of the United States;

7. disseminating information received from officers of the Department of Justice of the United States to subjects of investigations conducted by lawfully authorized investigative officers and employees of the United States, for the

purpose of aiding and assisting such subjects in their attempts to avoid criminal liability;

8. making or causing to be made false or misleading public statements for the purpose of deceiving the people of the United States into believing that a thorough and complete investigation had been conducted with respect to allegations of misconduct on the part of personnel of the executive branch of the United States and personnel of the Committee for the Re-election of the President, and that there was no involvement of such personnel in such misconduct: or

9. endeavouring to cause prospective defendants, and individuals duly tried and convicted, to expect favoured treatment and consideration in return for their silence or false testimony, or rewarding individuals for their silence or false testimony.

In all of this, Richard M. Nixon has acted in a manner contrary to his trust as President and subversive of constitutional government, to the great prejudice of the cause of law and justice and to the manifest injury of the people of the United States.

Wherefore Richard M. Nixon, by such conduct, warrants impeachment and trial, and removal from office.

(Adopted 27-11 by the Committee on the Judiciary of the House of Representatives, at 7.07pm on Saturday, 27th July, 1974, in Room 2141 of the Rayburn Office Building, Washington D.C.)

Article 2

Using the powers of the office of President of the United States, Richard M. Nixon, in violation of his constitutional oath faithfully to execute the office of President of the United States and, to the best of his ability, preserve, protect, and defend the Constitution of the United States, and in disregard of his constitutional duty to take care that the laws be faithfully executed, has repeatedly engaged in conduct violating the constitutional rights of citizens, impairing the due and proper administration of justice and the conduct of lawful inquiries, or contravening the laws governing agencies of the executive branch and the purposed of these agencies.

This conduct has included one or more of the following:

1. He has, acting personally and through his subordinates and agents, endeavoured to obtain from the Internal Revenue Service, in violation of the constitutional rights of citizens, confidential information contained in income tax returns for purposed not authorized by law, and to cause, in violation of the constitutional rights of citizens, income tax audits or other income tax investigations to be initiated or conducted in a discriminatory manner.

2. He misused the Federal Bureau of Investigation, the Secret Service, and other executive personnel, in violation or disregard of the constitutional rights of citizens, by directing or authorizing such agencies or personnel to conduct or continue electronic surveillance or other investigations for purposes unrelated to national security, the enforcement of laws, or any other lawful function of his office; he did direct, authorize, or permit the use of information obtained thereby for purposes unrelated to national security, the enforcement of laws, or any other lawful function of his office; and he did direct the concealment of certain records made by the Federal Bureau of Investigation of electronic surveillance.

3. He has, acting personally and through his subordinates and agents, in violation or disregard of the constitutional rights of citizens, authorized and permitted to be maintained a secret investigative unit within the office of the President, financed in part with money derived from campaign contributions, which unlawfully utilized the resources of the Central Intelligence Agency, engaged in covert and unlawful activities, and attempted to prejudice the constitutional right of an accused to a fair trial.

4. He has failed to take care that the laws were faithfully executed by failing to act when he knew or had reason to know that his close subordinates endeavoured to impede and frustrate lawful inquiries by duly constituted executive, judicial and legislative entities concerning the unlawful entry into the headquarters of the Democratic National Committee, and the cover-up thereof, and concerning other unlawful activities including those relating to the confirmation of Richard Kleindienst as Attorney General of the United States, the electronic surveillance of private citizens, the break-in into the offices of Dr. Lewis Fielding, and the campaign financing practices of the Committee to Re-elect the President.

5. In disregard of the rule of law, he knowingly misused the executive power by interfering with agencies of the executive branch, including the Federal Bureau of Investigation, the Criminal Division, and the Office of Watergate Special Prosecution Force, of the Department of Justice, and the Central Intelligence Agency, in violation of his duty to take care that the laws be faithfully executed.

In all of this, Richard M. Nixon has acted in a manner contrary to his trust as President and subversive of constitutional government, to the great prejudice of the cause of law and justice and to the manifest injury of the people of the United States.

Wherefore Richard M. Nixon, by such conduct, warrants impeachment and trial, and removal from office.

(Adopted __28-10__ by the Committee on the Judiciary of the House of Representatives.)

Article 3
In his conduct of the office of President of the United States, Richard M. Nixon, contrary to his oath faithfully to execute the office of President of the United States and, to the best of his ability, preserve, protect, and defend the Constitution of the United States, and in violation of his constitutional duty to take care that the laws be faithfully executed, has failed without lawful cause or excuse to produce papers and things as directed by duly authorized subpoenas issued by the Committee on the Judiciary of the House of Representatives on April 11, 1974, May 15, 1974, May 30, 1974, and June 24, 1974, and willfully disobeyed such subpoenas. The subpoenaed papers and things were deemed necessary by the Committee in order to resolve by direct evidence fundamental, factual questions relating to Presidential direction, knowledge or approval of actions demonstrated by other evidence to be substantial grounds for impeachment of the President. In refusing to produce these papers and things Richard M. Nixon, substituting his judgment as to what materials were necessary for the inquiry, interposed the powers of the Presidency against the lawful subpoenas of the House of Representatives, thereby assuming to himself functions and judgments necessary to the exercise of the sole power of impeachment vested by the Constitution in the House of Representatives.

In all of this, Richard M. Nixon has acted in a manner contrary to his trust as President and subversive of constitutional government, to the great prejudice of the cause of law and justice, and to the manifest injury of the people of the United States.

Wherefore, Richard M. Nixon, by such conduct, warrants impeachment and trial, and removal from office.

(Adopted 21-17 by the Committee on the Judiciary of the House of Representatives.)

AFTERWORD

Dear Reader,

OK, we've had a little fun spoofing the ideals of this administration and the people who support it. But all kidding aside, these folks are a serious threat to just about everything. Let's face it. George Bush is a troglodyte. He doesn't believe in evolution because he hasn't evolved beyond a brutish mentality—and that feeds into the type of person who supports this regime unconditionally. Who are they, these hard-core Bushies? Well, as it has been written, axes come in threes and here we certainly have an axis of the far religious right, dyed-in-the wool corporatists and blood and guts militarists. Those who fall into one or more of these categories are hopelessly lost. They are going to do everything they can to further this crazy agenda or fall on their swords trying and in George Bush they having a willing means to their ends. But while they form the unyielding base of support for the Republicans, the real power comes from the more moderate masses that for one reason or another still stick with the game plan. These are the folks that can possibly be reached. And, in fact, they must be reached, as they are really the *only* ones who can stop this mad assault on everything.

Why is that? The past two elections were very close races. The sides are pretty evenly matched but have tipped in slight favor of the Republicans. (No, not a mandate, you twits!) Now, hardly anyone who voted against Bush has flip-flopped to the dark side and morphed into an ardent admirer. So, with all things being equal, it looks very gloomy for the Dems or anyone slightly to the left of Rush Limbaugh having any chance of being elected in the future. But in truth, the great moderate middle is up for grabs.

Who are we talking about here? You've got your generational Republicans—people whose fathers voted Republican as did their grandfathers and so on as long as anyone in the family can remember. So they vote Republican out of sheer inertia. Then you've got your straight shooting conservative types who buy the Republican line about responsibility, honesty and integrity. You've got your sportsman or hunter who believes that the 2nd Amendment is safer in Republican hands. And don't forget the church folk, the hard working small businessman and just all sorts of average people all over the country. The point is, there is a great mass of people in this country who do believe in core values and are, in a manner of speaking, willfully blind to the fact that the Republicans no longer reflect their beliefs. So, the idea is to show them that their party has abandoned many of the principles they cherish and has gone over the deep end.

Now, you've got to be subtle and genuine if you're going to get your point across. Can you imagine going up to your sweet old granny and screaming, "Why are you voting for these crooks?!" Before you know it, that gentle old soul will have you in a vicious headlock and'll be cramming a bar of soap down your throat! Remember, you're talking to people who believe in fair play, frugality, family and church and have a somewhat pastoral view of life. You can't just come off like some crazed conspiracy theorist. Better you should say, "Grandma, I'm worried about the deficits that Mr. Bush is running. I always thought that the Republicans believed that you should balance budgets just like the way you run your home." OK—maybe you don't have to come across as an Eddie Haskell*, but you get the picture. [*From *Leave It To Beaver* fame. For those of you too young to remember, the Eddie Haskell character was a troublemaking bad boy who always put up a super phony front when talking to grown ups.]

Tact. That's the order of the day. In changing someone's mind you've got a load of preconceived notions and a whole lot of sheer bull to overcome. As most people get their news from the talking heads on TV, some of the things you want to talk about will be foreign to them. To say the least, this administration has gone to great lengths to either downplay certain facts or to disseminate false information outright. So, you have to go slow and challenge things point by point, not with a deluge of data. Don't go all over the map with the things that bother you. Rather, content yourself to focus on the subjects that concern the other person. Suppose, for example, you are confronted with the idea that Republicans respect the 2nd Amendment while the Democrats don't. Agree (in part). What else can you do? But you might take advantage of the conversation to slip in a plug for the 1st Amendment. "Sure," you reply, "Republicans make no secret about wanting to protect gun rights but let me ask you, don't you agree that the 1st Amendment is at least as important as the 2nd?" Having gained this concession (and maybe a "What's that got to do with anything?") you proceed by allowing that everyone agrees that there has to be limits put on free speech—the old "you can't yell fire in a crowded theater" idea. So why is it so hard to imagine that there should also be limits to firearms? Should Joe Six Pack be allowed to own a howitzer? You might then point out that Dick Cheney voted against banning cop killer bullets, against reasonable waiting periods and against restrictions on plastic, undetectable firearms—laws that passed during the Reagan and Bush presidencies. And he's hardly the most pro gun legislator today. In Florida, you now have the right to shoot first and ask questions later. It's one thing to protect the rights of gun owners but it's another to promote irresponsible ownership and greedy manufacturers.

Big government—invasive government—that's a big bugaboo with Conservatives. Yet there is no denying that Bush has created two new bureaucracies and consistently flip-flops on states' rights when it suits his purposes. And now that the Republicans have majorities in both houses we have for all intents and purposes a one party system. That's centralization (i.e., Communism!). But ask—what is the purpose of big government? The US government was not a huge monolith until the rise of big business. As companies merged and incredibly powerful monopolies came into existence it was necessary to counter their authority lest they begin to operate under their own rules. (Think about Enron and Halliburton—not to mention the close ties of these companies to the current administration—and their rapacious practices.) Sadly, big business simply cannot be trusted to put a leash on its worse tendencies. Thus it is up to the people to band together in the form of government to regulate and watch over every industry. Without a doubt, some bureaucracies become corrupt or swollen and overbearing but they, being under the control of the people can be brought to heel, *if* the people so wish it. Unfortunately, too many conservatives are letting this administration take power away from government to allow business to snoop more and more into our private lives. Also, at every turn they are appointing people with huge conflicts of interest to be our watchdogs. In Republican regimes, the fox is guarding the hen house in every nook and cranny. Is the profit motive more compelling to conservatives than the security, health and freedom of the American people? You betcha.

Most people are simply asleep at the switch. They get what little news they pay attention to from the talking heads of the mainstream media who dwell on everything but what is going on right in front of our faces. These folks generally say that whatever the administration is up to, it doesn't affect them. To these people I quote a famous poem:

First they came for the Communists, but I was not a Communist, so I said nothing. Then they came for the Social Democrats, but I was not a Social Democrat, so I did nothing. Then came the trade unionists, but I was not a trade unionist. And then they came for the Jews, but I was not a Jew, so I did little. Then when they came for me, there was no one left to stand up for me.

—Pastor Martin Niemoller (1892–1984)

How does one know how to target a particular subject? Easy. Just ask in a roundabout way. "What do you think are the most positive things to come out of this administration?" Whatever answer you get, it'll be the one most on that person's mind. So jump on that. You know the list:

1. Fiscal conservatism. Shoot that one right out of the water with the huge deficits Bush and his cronies are piling up.

2. Terrorism. What about it? The Bushies are creating more terrorists than anything else. 2004 marked a tripling of the amount of deaths attributed to terrorists over 2003 and 2005 is worse yet.

3. Government is the problem. It can't do anything. That's something of a total inconsistency since the people telling you this *are* the government and the people that believe it are eating out of their hands! So, we should let private companies take over the national weather service, vector control, port authorities, childhood services, welfare, rural postal delivery, etc.? Is industry going to fund all research and development? Get real.

4. National security. Are you feeling better now that we're pissing off every nation on earth? That we have an administration that is the most secretive ever, can't find Osama, hasn't improved airport security in years, underfunds the states in matters of security and is shown up by a bunch of yahoos without jobs guarding our southern borders?

5. Individual liberty. That's a hoot! Terry Schiavo—need we say more? The Republicans are constantly invading private space where *they* think they ought to be putting their noses. Now revelations of illegal wiretaps.

6. Responsibility. That is the biggest joke of all! Have you heard Bush take responsibility for anything that might have negative consequences? Or anybody in this administration? Ever? All we have ever heard is blaming *everything* on Clinton. Republicans are the biggest weasels in the world!

7. Tax relief. That's also a hoot unless you make gobs of money and maybe if you are so poor even this administration will stoop to give you a dime. But

the middle class is getting the holy hell squeezed out of it and you've been duped into cutting out estate taxes for multi-gazillionaires! Even if you did benefit a little, we ask, if we were to come and kill your neighbor, rape his wife, sell off the kids, torch the place and poison the lawn would you take a few bucks to keep silent? That's basically what you'd be doing.

8. Business. Bush likes to think of himself as America's CEO. We can see how running this country like a business is leaving it in shambles, especially if we've got a CEO who's a proven failure in business. The only thing Republicans know about business is how to get money into their political campaigns and then shovel the national treasure into their own pockets and the pockets of their donors. The blatant favors that they give help only a few targeted businesses to the detriment of everyone else. And this Social Security scheme in order to bail out Wall Street is just another scam they've cooked up. Wake up!

Wake up, indeed. There are no doubt other things on the list of former Republican values that this administration has thumbed its nose at. We leave it to you, dear reader, to complete the list.

Now, all this is not in any way shape or form a huge advertisement for the Democrats. One thing I used to tell my Republican amigos when they cried about Clinton (and they still do) was that it was in good measure the Republicans fault that he was in office. Oh, yeah! If George HW Bush hadn't been such a crappy President he would have hung on and won a second term. So, by the same token the Democrats—who should have easily defeated Bush both in 2000 and in 2004—showed up so lame as to lose *twice* to this maniac. So this is no glowing endorsement for the Dems. However, one must concede that they are the only game in town powerful enough to stem the tide of creeping fascism, theocracy and wanton warmongering. For a rallying cry I say, "Let there be gridlock!" A government frozen in partisan bickering is much preferable to a government unaccountable except to the Pat Robertsons, Ken Lays and John Boltons of America. Let's swing the pendulum of politics back to the midcourse, this time holding *all* parties' feet to the fire and not overlooking the excesses of either side. The powers that be use the left-right tension to divide and distract us all from the fact that we are being warred on by the wealthy and powerful. If we can set a middle course in our politics and truly marginalize the fringe left and right then perhaps we can unite a common front against the haves who play for keeps—that is, for keeping everything for themselves to the detriment of all mankind.

America used to be about helping oneself and not taking advantage of the powerless but that seems to have been supplanted by an I've-got-mine attitude and a mean spirited glee at the misery of others. While those that adhere to this mind-set look upon themselves as superior, in truth it is a clear sign of weakness and fear. So much macho nonsense really hides the fact that a frightened little creature is putting up a false front. The greater the bluster, the greater the hidden and denied fear beneath it all. So wake up America. Let's just say __no__ to these bullies and create a new world order that promotes life instead of the death loving "culture of life"—a new order that takes into account the value of human endeavors that favor peace, ecology and yes, love over the mere acquisition of money.

Not everything on the right is necessarily wrong. In fact, it is quite possible that two opposing views can both be right when looked at from differing points of view. For example, the argument against welfare usually asks the question, "Why should I be forced to fund that particular program?" That is, of course, an oversimplification but it is generally the root of the argument. And it is a fair question. Why should anyone be forced to contribute money to any particular cause? If we are going to have any kind of society we must pool our resources. The question is to what ends? The Constitution speaks of promoting the general welfare of the people but is not specific in that regard—at least not toward charity. So people who feel that they are forced to give their money to welfare have something of a legitimate argument. And one cannot simply counter by saying that they are forced to spend money on a military that they do not support since in the Constitution, there is specificity in that regard. My answer is that forced or not, we are morally bound to have at least a minimal assistance program for those who find themselves in dire need. There will be some who cheat the system but that is no cause for denying the whole thing. There will always be misuse in any system. Granted, in some cases there will be excess and some people will become dependent upon the system. Again, there will always be flaws but to dwell upon the rarer cases in order to condemn a whole program is flat out wrong. Nobody—except the out and out cheats—is getting rich on welfare. They never did and they never will. And this leads me to why I fall on the side of "forced" giving—the underlying reasons for not wanting to give to such programs are based on falsehoods. Ideas that there are legions of "welfare queens" and all sorts of undeserving people sponging off of the system are promulgated by the mean spirited. Myths are perpetuated in order to maintain a "moral" justification for sending a message of "tough love" by refusing to fund these programs. The same sort of right wing rumor mill gave cause for promoting the recent curtailments in bankruptcy law. They would have everyone believe that all who apply for bankruptcy are simply thieves who run up credit debt and then want to renege. The truth is that over 60% of such cases are because of overwhelming medical bills. Sure these people maxxed their credit cards in hopes of meeting their bills. That's a far cry from the idea that everyone is just trying to play the system. Sure there are cheats but these people can be easily exposed. But now, because of false propaganda we've got new laws that hurt average folks while forgiving the rich and powerful. Over and over the system is being gamed to favor those who already have to the exclusion and detriment of those who don't.

Listen closely to the talking heads and pundits on the right. They continually ascribe vile intentions and motives upon their foes. But people tend to view the world through their own personal lens. That is, they ascribe evil intent upon others because that is what *they* would do under the same circumstances.

How many on the right shrieked when Nelson Mandela assumed leadership in South Africa? They *knew* in their hearts that there was going to be a blood bath. Why? Because they knew that the blacks were sorely mistreated but more to the point, they knew that if the situations were reversed, they would seek bloody revenge. And yet it didn't happen.

As the Soviet Union unraveled under the orchestration of Mikhail Gorbachev, we continually heard the term *Glasnost*, meaning that they were faking the opening of their society. It was a clever trap. Soon, their evil plot would become obvious. And yet it didn't happen. Those who spoke of treachery, it would seem, speak out with treacherous hearts. No one is claiming that the Russians are now our bosom buddies. Deep suspicions abound and an uncertain future is looming. But without a shred of trust we can never hope to reconcile our differences.

So that is why I remain in the liberal camp. Liberals choose to believe that people respond in kind to kindness, that heroism is speaking truth to power and that the meek *shall* inherit the earth because openness is true strength.

> *"And so, to the end of history, murder shall breed murder, always in the name of right and honor and peace, until the gods are tired of blood and create a race that can understand."*
>
> —George Bernard Shaw

And finally, to all those hard-core for the New American Century: Just own it. It is so tiring hearing your apologies for this administration. Stop denying what is going on and just own it. Don't give us this crap about the Iraqis being better off now than under Saddam. You don't give a rat's ass for the Iraqis—you never did and you never will. Just come out and say that you approve of it all. Stop with excusing Bush and his cronies, claiming *they* were victims of flawed evidence. Just say you like the way they lied, cooking up the invasion and cherry picking "evidence" from all sorts of specious sources. Empire turns you on. Your entire self worth is tied up and invested in military might. Just own it. You like the slaughter. You were all for war from the very get-go. You don't care about the missing billions—to the victor goes the spoils. You don't care about under equipped troops, exposure to depleted uranium, stop loss, no WMD's, no exit strategy, Abu Ghraib and all the rest. The troops be damned—they should shut up and do as they are ordered.

Stop pretending that the facts are still in debate over deforestation, global warming, mercury and environmental links to cancer and other mental and physical diseases. Just own it. You simply don't care about the environment. Our economic standard of living is more important than anything else. No sacrifice is small enough to be considered.

Last but not least—to the religious right—no one cares what you believe and how you wish to run your life. Just leave the rest of us alone. Stop projecting your fears and weakness on others. If the fear of eternal damnation is the only thing that keeps you from being a psychopath then fine. But not everyone needs a threat to keep them in line. While you believe that everyone is born a hopeless sinner, corrupted by the sin of Adam it is *you* who gives credence to that belief. No one is suggesting that evil does not exist—it is within all of us. But it does not necessarily follow that the believer will not do evil and the unbeliever will. In point of fact it is human nature to obsess on strict taboos so stop trying to rid the world of everything you disapprove. Trying to rid the world of temptation and pretending that such things do not exist is just foolishness. If you don't want to do something, ignore it. If you can't stand the thought of other people doing it, pretend they don't—you are pretty good at pretending the folks you admire are living the straight and narrow. If you can't do that then take a pill.

978-0-595-38697

0-595-38697-0

Printed in the United States
46039LVS00003B/162

9 780595 386970